The ABA Checklist for Family Heirs

A Guide to Family History, Financial Plans and Final Wishes

SALLY BALCH HURME

AMERICAN BAR ASSOCIATION
Senior Lawyers
Division

Cover design by ABA Publishing

Page composition by Quadrum

The materials contained herein represent the opinions and views of the authors and/or the editors, and should not be construed to be the views or opinions of the law firms or companies with whom such persons are in partnership with, associated with, or employed by, nor of the American Bar Association or the Senior Lawyers Division, unless adopted pursuant to the bylaws of the Association.

Nothing contained in this book is to be considered as the rendering of legal advice for specific cases, and readers are responsible for obtaining such advice from their own legal counsel. This book and any forms and agreements herein are intended for educational and informational purposes only.

15 14 13   7 6

Library of Congress Cataloging-in-Publication Data

Hurme, Sally Balch.

The ABA checklist for family heirs : your guide to my family history, financial plans, and final wishes / By Sally Balch Hurme.

   p. cm.

ISBN 978-1-61632-852-8

1. Estate planning—United States. 2. Inheritance and succession—United States. 3. Wills—United States I. Title.

KF750.H87 2011

346.7305'2—dc22

2010053450

Discounts are available for books ordered in bulk. Special consideration is given to state bars, CLE programs, and other bar-related organizations. Inquire at Book Publishing, ABA Publishing, American Bar Association, 321 North Clark Street, Chicago, Illinois 60654.

www.ShopABA.org

TABLE OF CONTENTS

Chapter 2: Family History

Family History Checklist

Chapter 3: Insurance

Insurance Checklists

Investments Checklists

Chapter 7: Real Estate

Real Estate Checklists

Chapter 8: Other Assets and Debts

Other Assets and Debts Checklists

Chapter 9: Wills, Trust Agreements, and Powers of Attorney

Wills, Trust Agreements, and Powers of Attorney Checklists

Chapter 10: Final Wishes

Final Wishes Checklists

Appendix A: Checklists

Appendix B: Resources

ACKNOWLEDGMENTS

Thanks to Kathy Welton for suggesting that I really could and should take on writing this book and for lending a helping hand in getting me off to a good start.

My interest—no, call that my passion—for elder law came from my father, Joe Balch. He was the epitome of the elder law attorney long before anyone even called it elder law. I hope in some way I'm somewhat able to follow in his footsteps.

Hats go off to my sister Barbara, the queen of how to get things organized, who has already put to use many of these suggestions in her wonderful caring for our mother.

One test of this book's success will be when my husband heeds the book's advice. It's for our children Kirk and Kirsten and their children Kellen and Bridget that we assemble and organize this information. But the best result will be that you find it helpful.

ABOUT THE AUTHOR

Sally Balch Hurme, J.D.

Sally Balch Hurme, J.D., is currently a Senior Project Manager with the AARP Health Law Education team. In her nineteen years at AARP, she has advocated on a wide range of issues including consumer fraud, financial exploitation, elder abuse, surrogate decision making, advance care planning, predatory mortgage lending, health care fraud, and financial security. She is well recognized as an elder law advocate who is quoted frequently in national media including the *Wall Street Journal*, *USA Today*, CNN.com, *Money*, *Kiplinger's Retirement Report*, NPR, Sirius/XM Radio, and AARP The Magazine.

Although she has written over 20 law review articles on elder law topics, she has focused her professional career on explaining the law so everyone can understand it. She has lectured on elder abuse and surrogate decision making in the Netherlands, Germany, Spain, Italy, Czech Republic, Great Britain, and Moldova. In 2010, she delivered an Honor Lecture at the World Congress on Adult Guardianship in Yokohama, Japan. She is also in demand as a speaker having given over 100 presentations on elder law topics in at least 40 states.

For the past two decades her volunteer commitment has focused on the rights of adults with diminished capacity and the reform of guardianship policy and procedures. She has served multiple terms on the boards of the National Guardianship Association and the Center for Guardianship Certification, where she has been instrumental in developing standards for guardians and criteria to improve professional competency. Currently she serves as the chair of the National Guardianship Network, a collaboration of ten national organizations working to improve guardianship. She was an advisor to the Uniform Law Commission in the drafting of the uniform guardianship jurisdiction act which has been quickly adopted in 20 states. She was a member of U.S. State Department delegation to the Hague Conference on Private International Law that drafted the International Convention on the Protection of Incapacitated Adults. In 2008, she was honored by the National College of Probate Judges with the William Treat Award for excellence in probate law.

Hurme started her legal career as a partner in a private law firm, gained valuable experience serving older clients as a legal services attorney, and served as a magistrate in

Alexandria, Virginia. She spent three years as an attorney advisor with the U.S. Department of Justice Office of Intelligence Policy and Review. She then returned to elder law advocacy as an assistant staff attorney with the American Bar Association Commission on Law and Aging before moving to AARP. Hurme taught elder law as an adjunct professor at the George Washington University Law School for eight years, honing her ability to explain the law. She is a long-term member of the National Academy of Elder Law Attorneys and the Virginia and District of Columbia bars. Hurme is a member of the Discipline and Ethics Commission of the Certified Financial Planners Board of Standards. She is president of the Stuart Hall School Alumnae/I Council.

She received her B.A. from Newcomb College of Tulane University, New Orleans, Louisiana, and received her J.D. *cum laude* from the Washington College of Law, American University, Washington, D.C. She lives in Alexandria, VA, but enjoys get-away time at her farm near Shepardstown, WV.

INTRODUCTION:
MY GIFT TO YOU

To my heirs—

I have assembled this book for you. I am using the term "heirs" in the broadest sense. You are the people I care about and who care about me. You may be my spouse, my children or grandchildren, or special friends or loved ones who may not be directly related to me.

By providing my personal history in Chapter 1 and my family history in Chapter 2, I wish to share with those who will follow me my memories and knowledge of those who came before me.

By detailing my assets and benefits in Chapters 3-8, I hope to ease the process of handling my estate and make you aware of all resources to which you may be entitled. In Chapter 4 you will find useful checklists to aid you in applying for any benefits to which you may be entitled. In the other chapters in this section I've recorded much of the information you will need to know about what assets and liabilities I have. I have done this as my gift to you so that after my death you will be able to more easily know what I have and be able to locate the important documentation you will need.

In describing my final wishes in Chapters 9 and 10, I hope to spare you difficult decisions you might otherwise need to make on my behalf. The information about powers of attorney for both my financial affairs and my medical decisions will come into play in the event I become incapacitated. You will find information about my instructions to the persons I have given the authority and responsibility to make decisions on my behalf when I cannot make those decisions on my own. In Chapter 10 I have set out what I would like for you to do upon my death. The Survivors Checklist gives you, my immediate family, some of the steps that you will need to take in the first few days and weeks after I die.

I hope that this book brings you comfort and peace of mind. My gratitude and thanks to you for your kind attention to my final wishes.

To the user of this book—

One of the kindest things you can do for your family is to spare them needless frustrations and stressful decisions at the time of your death. Many people live together for 50 years without discussing their wishes regarding life support, organ donations, funeral or memorial services, and burial or cremation. Without meaning to do so, they leave many distressing decisions for their loved ones. You can make your own death easier on your family and significant others by simply deciding on and recording your own preferences.

Having an up-to-date will is an important step in your planning. A will, however, is not the place for detailing such wishes or recording all the information your family needs to know, because it only directs the distribution of your property after your death. Most wills simply divide estates into bulk portions, mentioning major assets and leaving heirs, executors, and the courts to determine what else is included in the deceased's estate. Without clear records, the family is faced with the burdensome and often costly task of locating records, papers, and documents to establish the content and value of the estate.

Perhaps even more important to you and to your family is the cherished legacy you can provide your heirs by passing on your unique knowledge of your family history, your recollections about your own life, interests, and accomplishments, and other special remembrances.

How to use this book

This book is divided into three sections. In the first section you can record information about you and your family. Next are checklists where you can compile information about your personal assets and property. In the final section you can assemble information that can alleviate some of the burdens your family could face if you become incapacitated and at the time of your death. This provides you a place to express your final wishes.

Each chapter starts with a checklist you can use to collect the information you want to gather. For each item on the checklist you will find an explanation why you might want to pass on this information and how to organize it if you have not yet done so. You will find checklists designed for you to provide your heirs with a detailed personal record of your assets, family history, personal history, final wishes, and other notes. The chapters end with additional checklists your family can use as they carry out your wishes and assume the responsibilities you have given to them. They will even find suggestions as to how they can help you assemble some of the information for this project, if you want their assistance.

It is most unlikely that you will be able to complete this guide in one or two sittings. Some information will take extra thought or research. But don't look upon it as a task. If you approach it in manageable sections and view it as a fascinating family project, you will find it can give you great satisfaction to track down bits and pieces of your family history, locate the missing birth certificates, and gradually put your affairs in order.

You will probably want to start by looking through the Checklist of Checklists on page 230 to get an overview of the many topics covered by this book. Go through a first run to check off the items that don't apply to your circumstances. If so, indicate that they do not and move on. You may find that you'll want to start with just one section or checklist that is the easiest for you to accomplish.

Check off each item on the lists as you complete that step. Even though you might not have all the answers at first, take the time to find them. You will find tips on how to gather some of the information and places to record your information. You know the sources; your heirs may not.

You should also prioritize the things that you want to complete sooner rather than later. Your priority list is unique to you but some things that you will want to put at the top of your list include having medical advance directives, recording your personal medication record, filing in your personal history, talking with your attorney about your estate plans, indicating where your important papers are located, and making decisions about your funeral.

You are never too young or too old to make plans and arrangements so you can stay in control of your affairs. Accidents, strokes, heart attacks and dementia can happen at any age. By starting now to plan ahead for possible incapacity and inevitable death you are taking the positive steps to getting your life in order, reaching peace of mind, and ensuring your wishes are known.

Feel free to modify the checklists according to your needs. For example, if you are unmarried but have someone significant in your life that you would like to include, just cross through *spouse* and replace it with the term you prefer to describe your relationship, such as *special friend* or *lifetime partner*.

Fill in the paper checklists with a pencil. This is book for you to write in. If your decisions or assets change as time goes by, it will be easy to erase what you have previously written and insert new financial information or personal directions for your heirs.

Print legibly. After all, if you take the time to organize this record for your heirs, you want them to be able to read it.

Keep the forms up-to-date. As changes occur, update the forms. Update and review them at least once per year. Schedule a month or two at the beginning of each year to update the forms and add new information. Just after you have pulled together files and papers to prepare your taxes is a good time to review and update these forms.

Utilize the CD-ROM. The checklists in this book are included electronically on a CD-ROM for use on your computer. This makes it very easy for you to fill out the checklists and to make changes so they are up-to-date. Note in this book the file or folder name so your heirs can easily find it on your computer. As you complete a chapter you may want to print out a copy and place the pages in a three-ring binder. You may also want to add plastic pages into which you can put clippings, or papers when you come across them. You'll want to keep a hard copy (and a backup file) of these documents in your filing system. Be sure to note where you have those copies stored so they will be readily available to your heirs.

Discuss this book with your heirs. They must be aware that you have taken the time to gather the valuable information in this book, know where your checklists are located, and know what it says in order for it to be of value to them. Be sure to let them know that you are working on gathering this information. Whether you are recording this information in the book, storing the information electronically or are printing out pages for a binder, your family needs to know how to locate this treasure trove of information.

A word of caution. You are assembling a great deal of very personal information that, in the wrong hands, could be used to your disadvantage. Unfortunately, there are unscrupulous people who do not have your best interests in mind. They may even be people you think you should be able to trust. While they may not admit it, some relatives may be more concerned about their own interests than in yours. In some families, it is difficult to impossible to reach a consensus or agreement about just about anything. Be cautious about with whom you share the information you're collecting. The nosy neighbor, the distant relative, or the casual friend may not be able to keep confidential this very private information.

A word of encouragement. These records can be of great interest and value to you during your lifetime and can provide a sense of great freedom. The greatest satisfaction will be in knowing that if anything happens to you, you will be providing an invaluable resource for your heirs with your notes, your wishes, and the information in this book.

CHAPTER 1
PERSONAL HISTORY

We can only be said to be alive in those moments
when our hearts are conscious of our treasures.

—Thornton Wilder

No one knows your personal history as well as you do. Chances are good that your children, family, and significant others may not know as much about you as you might think. Even if some of your immediate family does know all about your personal history, you'll find many benefits to taking the time to record the details. You can make sure that the information passed on to later generations is accurate. Not only will they benefit from this information, you may also enjoy tracking down bits of information and remembering key events in your life.

- Where you were born
- Where you went to school
- Where you have lived
- The different types of work experiences you have had
- The hobbies and activities you have enjoyed through the years

And yet, haven't you asked yourself many of these questions in regard to your parents? Or your grandparents? Or your brothers and sisters? Most of us become more interested in family history as we grow older, but if someone does not record that history for us, it will be lost. *You* are the one who can do this best for your heirs.

My Checklist

Done   **Need to Do**

Done	Need to Do	
☐	☐	Get copies of birth certificate
☐	☐	Get copies of marriage license
☐	☐	Get copies of divorce decree
☐	☐	Complete Personal Medication Record
☐	☐	Organize tax files by year
☐	☐	List all employers
☐	☐	Keep original documents that are valuable or irrplaceable in a safe deposit box
☐	☐	Complete the checklists for Chapter 1

Personal History Checklists

The checklists in Chapter 1 are set out in the following order:

- *Awards*
- *Biography*
- *Contacts*
- *Educational History*
- *Memberships*
- *Passwords*
- *Personal Medication Record*
- *Pets*
- *Records*
- *Religion, Politics, and Hobbies*
- *Residences*
- *Taxes*
- *Work History*
- *Personal History: Other*

The checklists in Chapter 1 seek more detailed information about you—your educational background, where you have lived and worked, organizations you have joined, and your awards, pets, religion, politics, and hobbies.

On the Contacts Checklist you can put in one convenient place the contact information for all the people you rely on, and with whom your family may need to get in touch. You should have fun filling out the Records Checklist pages. Just where have you located the keys to your safe deposit box and what's the combination for the lock on your extra storage shed? Let someone know where you are keeping important papers. You never know when your family will need to find a copy of your contract for your security system or your homeowner's insurance policy. In other chapters you can record more information about these various documents.

Finally, you will find a page entitled "Other." This is for *you* to fill in with personal notes about yourself—your interests, accomplishments, thoughts, or desires. Add anything you consider to be of interest to your family and heirs. Don't be modest! If you did something in your lifetime for which you are proud, tell them about it. They will be proud, too. If something very humorous happened to you, your heirs will enjoy it. Remember how you were fascinated with the interesting stories told to you by your mother, father, and grandparents? Your heirs are just as interested in your remembrances.

A primary purpose of the checklists in Chapter 1 is to provide enjoyment for your heirs. However, there are other purposes. At the time of death, some of this information can be used in the preparation of a death certificate, newspaper obituary, tax returns, income tax returns, and many other administrative forms, as well as applying for survivors' benefits.

✔ **Get copies of birth certificate**

✔ **Get copies of marriage license**

You want now to locate your own birth and marriage certificates. Your family is going to need these documents to settle your estate and apply for various benefits. You need to record where you have stored your certificates or start the process now to obtain copies. While you are tracking down your own certificates, you may also want to obtain copies of certificates for your family members. It is a good idea to request them now so they will always be on hand.

The vast majority of births, deaths, and marriages are reported to the proper authorities to maintain a lasting record. However, for a number of reasons, your heirs may have difficulty or encounter delay obtaining these records if you have not put them where they can readily find them. For example, in the not too distant past, many births occurred in private homes and went unrecorded. Occasionally, fire destroys courthouses or other record depositories. Records may be incorrect because of misspelling, changes in spelling, illegible handwriting, misunderstanding of names, and other errors.

Obtain and keep in a safe-deposit box two *certified* copies each of your birth certificate, your spouse's birth certificate, your marriage certificate, and the birth certificates of your children. To be "certified copy" it must have a statement by official that it is a true copy of an original.

Each state has its own method of maintaining these records. They can usually be obtained from the county clerk, registrar, or recorder of the county in which the birth or marriage took place.

Many states have a central clearing house generally called the Department of Vital Statistics. The Centers for Disease Control and Prevention has a useful website with information on how and where to write to obtain these records in each state at www.cdc.gov/nchs/w2w.htm.

To expedite the sometimes lengthy procedure of obtaining the certificates it is a good idea first to find out how much each certificate will cost. Fees generally range from $2 to $20. Additional copies may be available at reduced rates. Once you know the cost, you can write for the copies you need, enclosing the necessary payment.

Many states will not issue copies of birth or marriage certificates unless the requestor is closely related to the person named in the certificate. Therefore, it is important to identify yourself as spouse, parent or child, when requesting records for someone else in your family.

✔ Get copies of divorce decree

Your family will also need certified copies of judgments of divorce or annulment to apply for death or survivor Social Security benefits, veterans benefits, and private pension plans. You obtain them from the clerk or registrar of the court that granted the divorce or annulment. Once again, the fee for obtaining copies varies in each state and may also depend upon the number of pages in the document.

Write a letter to the court that granted the decree or judgment to inquire about the cost of obtaining a copy of the document. Note the date and year the divorce or annulment was granted, and be sure to enclose a self-addressed, stamped envelope.

✔ Complete Personal Medication Record

Carrying with you at all times a record of the medications you are taking can be life-saving. If you should have a sudden illness, emergency responders and your family need to know promptly what medications you have been taken, any medical conditions for which you are receiving treatment and any allergies you might have.

You should complete the Personal Medication Record to keep track of all your medications. Be sure to list your prescription drugs, as well as any over-the-counter drugs, herbal or dietary supplements, and vitamins. You should include the name of the drug as well as the reason you are taking it. If you are not sure why your doctor prescribed a medication, ask your doctor. You can also list the form of the medication, such as whether it is a pill, liquid, patch or injection. Also record the dosage. This would be, for example, how many milligrams in each tablet. Note how much you are supposed to take and how frequently; for example, "one pill at breakfast." In the last column, you can include any special directions, such as "with food."

Carry a copy with you all the time. You should also share this information with your doctors and pharmacists during each appointment. Also make sure that a family member knows what medications you are taking.

✔ Organize tax files by year

Your past tax returns can be an invaluable source of information that your executor or personal representative may need to know. Your executor will be responsible for filing your income tax return for the year of your death. Your executor will also need to prepare any estate tax returns. If your recent returns and the supporting documentation for any schedules or itemized deductions are readily located, you can save your executor much time and frustration.

✔ List all employers

By listing all your past employers, your executor will be able to quickly determine places to check about any benefits, pensions, retirement accounts, insurance benefits, or even unpaid leave that might be available for your heirs.

✔ Keep original documents that are valuable or irreplaceable in a safe deposit box

In the Records Checklist starting on page 24 you should list where you are keeping many of your records, lists, and documents. You can check off the items that are in your safe deposit box or note where you are storing other information, including copies of all the checklists in this book. Only the most important documents need to be kept in your safe deposit. Information that you want to update frequently or need ready access to doesn't need to be locked away in your safe deposit box. However, you will want to note on this checklist where you are keeping things that are not in your safe deposit box.

To my heirs:

Because I know that you will undoubtedly need copies of my birth, marriage, and divorce papers I have obtained certified copies to save you the time and trouble to obtain them. You will find them located _____

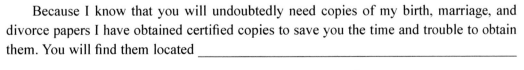

_____.

It took me some doing to collect all the other information in this chapter but I know that it will be valuable to you in many different ways, if for no other reason than you'll get to know my personal story.

Heirs Checklist

✔ Offer to help to track down information, organize mementos, or create scrapbooks.

✔ Assist with keeping the Personal Medical Record up-to-date as medications change.

CHAPTER 1
PERSONAL HISTORY CHECKLISTS

Awards

I received the following academic awards and scholarships:

_____
_____
_____
_____
_____
_____
_____
_____

I received the following athletic awards and scholarships:

_____
_____
_____
_____
_____
_____
_____
_____

I received the following work-related awards and commendations:

_____

_____

_____

_____

_____

_____

_____

_____

Biography

The following describes my biography:

_____

_____

_____

_____

_____

_____

_____

_____

_____

_____

_____

_____

_____

_____

_____

_____

_____

_____

_____

_____

_____

_____

_____

_____

_____

_____

_____

_____

_____

_____

_____

Contacts

Financial Advisors

Accountant: _____

Phone: _____ Email: _____

Address: _____

_____

Attorney: _____

Phone: _____ Email: _____

Address: _____

_____

Banker: _____

Phone: _____ Email: _____

Address: _____

_____

Executor: _____

Phone: _____ Email: _____

Address: _____

_____

Insurance Agent: _____

Phone: _____ Email: _____

Address: _____

_____

Investment Advisor: _____

Phone: _____ Email: _____

Address: _____

_____

Tax Advisor: _____

Phone:_____ Email: _____

Address: _____

_____

Other: _____

Phone:_____ Email: _____

Address: _____

_____

Medical Professionals

Primary Physician: _____

Phone:_____ Email: _____

Address: _____

_____

Specialty Physician: _____

Phone:_____ Email: _____

Address: _____

_____

Specialty Physician: _____

Phone:_____ Email: _____

Address: _____

_____

Dentist: _____

Phone:_____ Email: _____

Address: _____

_____

Other: _____

Phone:_____ Email: _____

Address: _____

_____

Service Providers

Children's Babysitter: _____

Phone:_____ Email: _____

Address: _____

_____

Children's Dentist: _____

Phone:_____ Email: _____

Address: _____

_____

Children's Physician: _____

Phone:_____ Email: _____

Address: _____

_____

Children's School/Daycare: _____

Phone:_____ Email: _____

Address: _____

_____

Housekeeper:_____

Phone:_____ Email: _____

Address: _____

_____

Lawn Service/Gardener: _____

Phone:_____ Email: _____

Address: _____

_____

Maintenance:_____

Phone:_____ Email: _____

Address: _____

_____

Pet's Veterinarian: _____

Phone:_____ Email: _____

Address: _____

_____

Property Manager: _____

Phone:_____ Email: _____

Address: _____

_____

Security System: _____

Phone:_____ Email: _____

Address: _____

_____

Other: _____

Phone:_____ Email: _____

Address: _____

_____

Educational History

I attended the following elementary or grade schools:

Name of School	Location	Grades Attended	Dates Attended

I attended the following high schools, junior high schools, or middle schools:

Name of School	Location	Grades Attended	Dates Attended

I attended the following preparatory schools:

Name of School	Location	Grades Attended	Dates Attended

I attended the following colleges or universities:

Name of Institution	Location	Dates Attended/ Graduated	Degrees/ Certificates

I attended the following additional schools and training programs:

Name of Institution/ Training Program	Location	Dates Attended/ Graduated	Degrees/ Certificates

I was involved in the following extracurricular activities (art, athletic, debate, drama, fraternity, music, school newspaper, sorority, etc.):

_____

_____

_____

_____

_____

_____

_____

_____

_____

_____

_____

Memberships

I belong to the following organizations:

Membership Organization: _____

Phone: _____ Website: _____

Address: _____

_____

Involvement: _____

Interesting Facts: _____

_____

_____

Membership Organization: _____

Phone: _____ Website: _____

Address: _____

_____

Involvement: _____

Interesting Facts: _____

_____

_____

Membership Organization: _____

Phone: _____ Website: _____

Address: _____

_____

Involvement: _____

Interesting Facts: _____

_____

_____

Membership Organization: _____

Phone: _____ Website: _____

Address: _____

_____

Involvement: _____

Interesting Facts: _____

_____

_____

Membership Organization: _____

Phone: _____ Website: _____

Address: _____

_____

Involvement: _____

Interesting Facts: _____

_____

_____

Passwords

I have the following passwords:

Organization	User Name	Password	Website URL

Organization	User Name	Password	Website URL

Organization	User Name	Password	Website URL

Organization	User Name	Password	Website URL

Organization	User Name	Password	Website URL

Organization	User Name	Password	Website URL

Organization	User Name	Password	Website URL

Organization	User Name	Password	Website URL

Organization	User Name	Password	Website URL

Organization	User Name	Password	Website URL

Organization	User Name	Password	Website URL

Organization	User Name	Password	Website URL

Organization	User Name	Password	Website URL

Organization	User Name	Password	Website URL

Organization	User Name	Password	Website URL

Personal Medication Record

My Personal Information:

Name: _____

Date of Birth: _____

Phone Number: _____

Emergency Contact:

Name: _____

Relationship: _____

Phone Number: _____

Primary Care Physician:

Name: _____

Phone Number: _____

Pharmacy/Drugstore:

Name: _____

Pharmacist: _____

Phone Number: _____

Other Physicians:

Name: _____

Specialty: _____

Phone Number: _____

Name: _____

Specialty: _____

Phone Number: _____

My Medical Conditions:

_____

_____

_____

_____

_____

_____

_____

_____

_____

_____

My Allergies:

_____

_____

_____

_____

_____

_____

What	Reason	Form	Dosage	When	Notes

Be sure to include *all* prescription drugs, over-the-counter drugs, vitamins, and herbal or dietary supplements.

Pets

I own the following pets:

Pet Name/ Type	Species/ Coloring	Date of Birth	Date of Ownership	Food, Water, Care, and Exercise	Veterinarian

Pet Name/ Type	Species/ Coloring	Date of Birth	Date of Ownership	Food, Water, Care, and Exercise	Veterinarian

Pet Name/ Type	Species/ Coloring	Date of Birth	Date of Ownership	Food, Water, Care, and Exercise	Veterinarian

Pet Name/ Type	Species/ Coloring	Date of Birth	Date of Ownership	Food, Water, Care, and Exercise	Veterinarian

Pet Name/ Type	Species/ Coloring	Date of Birth	Date of Ownership	Food, Water, Care, and Exercise	Veterinarian

Pet Name/ Type	Species/ Coloring	Date of Birth	Date of Ownership	Food, Water, Care, and Exercise	Veterinarian

(See page 220 describing my wishes for the further care and placement of my pets.)

Records

For each record or item indicate whether you have it stored in your safe deposit box or another location. Obviously not everything needs to be or even should be stored in a safe deposit box. Other secure places could be a fire-proof box, filing cabinet, electronic file or in this book. It's important to let your family know where you have placed these items for safe keeping.

Safe Deposit Box	Record Type	Other Location
	Personal History	
☐	Adoption papers	_____
☐	Animal care information	_____
☐	Annulment decrees or judgments	_____
☐	Appointment book or calendar	_____
☐	Athletic awards	_____
☐	Award certificates	_____
☐	Birth certificates	_____
☐	Change of name certificates	_____
☐	Child care information	_____
☐	Civic awards	_____
☐	Divorce decrees or judgments	_____
☐	Dramatic awards	_____
☐	Drivers license	_____
☐	Educational awards	_____
☐	Educational certificates	_____
☐	Educational transcripts	_____
☐	Employment awards	_____

Safe Deposit Box	Record Type	Other Location
☐	Keys to residence	_____
☐	Keys to post office box	_____
☐	Keys to safe deposit box	_____
☐	Keys to vehicles	_____
☐	Keys to other real estate	_____
☐	Lock combinations	_____
☐	Membership awards	_____
☐	Membership certificates	_____
☐	Military awards	_____
☐	Military separation papers	_____
☐	Music/CDs catalog	_____
☐	Naturalization papers	_____
☐	Other awards	_____
☐	Passport	_____
☐	Passwords	_____
☐	Photo albums	_____
☐	Photos	_____
☐	Property care information	_____
☐	Security system information	_____
☐	Tax returns and records	_____
☐	Timeshare records	_____
☐	Videos/Movies catalog	_____
☐	Other	_____

Safe Deposit Box	Record Type	Other Location
☐	Other	_____
☐	Other	_____
	Family History	
☐	Adoption papers	_____
☐	Birth certificates	_____
☐	Marriage certificates	_____
☐	Newspaper articles	_____
☐	Photo albums	_____
☐	Portraits	_____
☐	Family tree	_____
☐	Other	_____
☐	Other	_____
☐	Other	_____
	Insurance Policies	
☐	Annuities	_____
☐	Automobile	_____
☐	Life	_____
☐	Long-term care	_____
☐	Medical	_____
☐	Medicare card	_____
☐	Medicare Part D	_____
☐	Residence	_____
☐	Umbrella	_____

Safe Deposit Box	Record Type	Other Location
☐	Other	_____
☐	Other	_____
☐	Other	_____
	Benefits	
☐	401 (k) agreements	_____
☐	403 (b) agreements	_____
☐	Disability agreements	_____
☐	IRA agreements	_____
☐	Keogh plan agreements	_____
☐	Military separation papers	_____
☐	Pension agreements	_____
☐	SEP agreements	_____
☐	Social Security card	_____
☐	Social Security Benefit Statement	_____
☐	Workers' compensation	_____
☐	Other	_____
☐	Other	_____
☐	Other	_____
	Banking and Savings	
☐	Checking account statements	_____
☐	Credit union account statements	_____
☐	Savings account statements	_____

Safe Deposit Box	Record Type	Other Location
☐	Other	_____
☐	Other	_____
☐	Other	_____
	Investments	
☐	Brokerage account statements	_____
☐	Certificates of Deposit	_____
☐	Savings Bonds	_____
☐	Other	_____
☐	Other	_____
☐	Other	_____
	Real Estate	
☐	Deeds	_____
☐	Home improvement records	_____
☐	Land contracts	_____
☐	Leases	_____
☐	Mortgages	_____
☐	Reverse mortgage	_____
☐	Tax records	_____
☐	Timeshare agreements	_____
☐	Other	_____
☐	Other	_____
☐	Other	_____

Safe Deposit Box	Record Type	Other Location
	Other Assets and Debts	
☐	Business records	_____
☐	Computers	_____
☐	Copyrights	_____
☐	Collectibles	_____
☐	Credit card contracts	_____
☐	Jewelry appraisals	_____
☐	Jewelry inventory	_____
☐	Patents and trademarks	_____
☐	Rare books	_____
☐	Vehicles	_____
☐	Vehicle certificates of title	_____
☐	Warranties	_____
☐	Websites	_____
☐	Other	_____
☐	Other	_____
☐	Other	_____
	Estate Planning	
☐	Durable power of attorney	_____
☐	Trust agreement	_____
☐	Will and codicils	_____
☐	Other	_____

Safe Deposit Box	Record Type	Other Location
☐	Other	_____
☐	Other	_____
	Final Wishes	
☐	Body bequeathal papers	_____
☐	Celebration of life prearrangements	_____
☐	Cemetery deed	_____
☐	Cremation prearrangement agreement	_____
☐	Ethical Will/Legacy documents	_____
☐	Funeral prearrangement agreement	_____
☐	Health care directives	_____
☐	Legacy information	_____
☐	Letters to be sent	_____
☐	Living will	_____
☐	Mausoleum deed	_____
☐	Pet continuing care	_____
☐	People to contact	_____
☐	Uniform donor card	_____
☐	Other	_____
☐	Other	_____
☐	Other	_____

Religion, Politics, and Hobbies

My religious activities and beliefs are as follows:

_____

_____

_____

_____

_____

_____

_____

_____

My politics are as follows:

_____

_____

_____

_____

_____

_____

_____

My hobbies are as follows:

_____

_____

_____

_____

_____

_____

_____

Residences

I lived in the following cities and states at the addresses listed below:

Address	City	State	Dates

Address	City	State	Dates

Address	City	State	Dates

Address	City	State	Dates

Address	City	State	Dates

Address	City	State	Dates

Address	City	State	Dates

Taxes

I pay the following taxes:

- ☐ Business
- ☐ Federal
- ☐ Personal Property
- ☐ Real Estate
- ☐ State
- ☐ Other

Tax Type	$ Amount	Frequency	Accountant	Notes

Tax Type	$ Amount	Frequency	Accountant	Notes

Tax Type	$ Amount	Frequency	Accountant	Notes

Tax Type	$ Amount	Frequency	Accountant	Notes

Tax Type	$ Amount	Frequency	Accountant	Notes

Tax Type	$ Amount	Frequency	Accountant	Notes

Work History

☐ I am presently employed at the following company and job listed below:

Name of Employer	Location/Phone #	Dates	Type of Work/ Job Title

I worked at the following companies and jobs listed below:

Name of Employer	Location/Phone #	Dates	Type of Work/ Job Title

Name of Employer	Location/Phone #	Dates	Type of Work/ Job Title

Name of Employer	Location/Phone #	Dates	Type of Work/ Job Title

Name of Employer	Location/Phone #	Dates	Type of Work/ Job Title

Name of Employer	Location/Phone #	Dates	Type of Work/ Job Title

Name of Employer	Location/Phone #	Dates	Type of Work/ Job Title

Name of Employer	Location/Phone #	Dates	Type of Work/ Job Title

☐ I retired from work on: _____

Date

The following describe accomplishments and interesting projects concerning my employment and may be of interest to my heirs:

_____

_____

_____

_____

_____

_____

_____

_____

_____

_____

_____

_____

_____

_____

_____

_____

Personal History: Other

The following miscellaneous information about me may be of interest to my heirs:

_____

_____

_____

_____

_____

_____

_____

_____

_____

_____

_____

_____

_____

_____

_____

_____

_____

_____

_____

_____

_____

_____

_____

_____

_____

_____

CHAPTER 2
FAMILY HISTORY

*The golden moments in the stream of life rush past us
and we see nothing but sand; the angels come to visit
us, and we only know them when they are gone.*

—George Eliot

Information that you know about your parents and grandparents could easily be lost. With each passing generation it becomes harder to track down when a distant relative settled in this country or where a favorite grandparent is buried.

My Checklist

Done	Need to Do	
☐	☐	Take advantage of family gatherings or reunions to get help compiling family history information
☐	☐	Complete the Family Medical History
☐	☐	Complete the checklists for Chapter 2

Go through the checklists in Chapter 2 and fill in as many answers as you can. You may have many blanks when you finish. Make gathering the rest of the answers an enjoyable project. Telephone, drop a note, or email your parent, brother, sister, aunt, uncle, son, or daughter and gradually complete your personal history. As a bonus, you may even rekindle family ties.

Family History Checklist

The checklists in Chapter 2 are set out in the following order:

- *Personal History*
- *Children*
- *Parents*
- *Brothers and Sisters*
- *Grandparents*
- *Aunts, Uncles, and Cousins*
- *Stepparents*
- *Stepbrothers and sisters*
- *Family Medical History*
- *Family History: Other*

In all the other chapters the checklists are in alphabetical order, but in this chapter they are listed according to how they might inherit if you do not have a will. This is called intestate succession. You'll learn more about this in chapter 9.

Checklists are provided for multiple spouses, children, and siblings. Please feel free to add more lines or to modify them to suit your needs. For example, if you are unmarried but have someone significant you would like to include, simply cross through *spouse* and replace it with the term you prefer to describe your relationship, such as *lifetime partner* or *special friend.*

You have space to write personal notes about your relatives. Use the space as you wish. For example, you can give a brief history, explain their beliefs or accomplishments, or share personal reminiscences. Here is a place to pass on those special moments you shared with a grandparent or the funny story about your brother when you were kids.

While you are searching out information about your relatives, this is a good time to note when and where they were born, as well as when they died and the cause of death. This information may be recorded on birth certificates and on death certificates, respectively. Census records, obituaries in newspapers, and online genealogical sites can also be helpful resources to track down missing information about your ancestors.

✔ Complete the Family Medical History

By completing the Family Medical History Checklist, you will be sharing information that may prove valuable in the diagnosis, early treatment, and, in some cases, prevention of certain hereditary medical conditions. You and your family can use this information to see if there are common illnesses or medical conditions in your family. This will help your family identify possible risks for certain diseases and ways to reduce or prevent those risks in the future.

You'll probably need to work with other family members in filling out the family medical history checklist. Keep in mind that some family members may not be willing, and may even be hostile, to share this personal information. You will need to respect the privacy of anyone who is not comfortable revealing health information.

Heirs Checklist

✔ Help dig into family history by offering to sort through photographs, letters, trunks and boxes in the attic.

✔ Try out some of the genealogical resources online to map out family trees.

✔ Offer to record on tape or video special memories to preserve oral family stories.

CHAPTER 2
FAMILY HISTORY CHECKLISTS

Personal History

Name: _____

First   Middle   Last

Name at Birth:_____

First   Middle   Last

Place of Birth: _____

City   State   Country

Date of Birth: _____

Legal Name Change:_____

First   Middle   Last

Legal Name Change Date: _____

Legal Name Change Court: _____

Court   City   State

****

Current Address: _____

_____

How Many Years: _____

Phone: _____ Cell Phone: _____

Fax: _____ Email:_____

****

Occupation or Industry: _____

How Many Years: _____

****

Citizenship: _____

    ☐ By Birth

    ☐ By Naturalization

Naturalization Date: _____

    ☐ Naturalization Place: _____

                                        City   *State*   *Country*

****

Military Veteran:

    ☐ Yes

    ☐ No

Branch of Service: _____

Dates of Service: _____

Serial #: _____ Rank: _____

Type of Discharge: _____

****

Social Security #: _____

Passport #: _____ Expiration: _____

Country of Issue: _____

Drivers License #: _____ Expiration: _____

State of Issue: _____

****

Marital Status:

    ☐ Divorced

    ☐ Married

    ☐ Never Married

    ☐ Widowed

First Spouse

Name of Spouse at Birth: _____

Date of Birth: _____

Place of Birth: _____

Date of Marriage: _____

Date of Divorce: _____

Date of Death: _____

Spouse is buried at: _____

Cause of death: _____

Name at present: _____

Phone: _____ Fax: _____

Address: _____

_____

Second Spouse

Name of Spouse at Birth: _____

Date of Birth: _____

Place of Birth: _____

Date of Marriage: _____

Date of Divorce: _____

Date of Death: _____

Spouse is buried at: _____

Cause of death: _____

Name at present: _____

Phone: _____ Fax: _____

Address: _____

_____

Third Spouse

Name of Spouse at Birth: _____

Date of Birth: _____

Place of Birth: _____

Date of Marriage: _____

Date of Divorce: _____

Date of Death: _____

Spouse is buried at: _____

Cause of death: _____

Name at present: _____

Phone: _____ Fax: _____

Address: _____

_____

Children

Name at present: _____

Phone: _____ Fax: _____

Address: _____

_____

Email: _____

Favorite memories:

_____

_____

_____

Name at birth: _____

Place of birth: _____

City   County   State   Country

Child is buried at: _____

Cause of death: _____

☐ Child has never been married.

☐ Child is currently married.

☐ Child has been married _____ times.

	Name of Spouse	Date of Marriage	Date of Divorce	Date of Death
# 1				
# 2				
# 3				

☐ Child has not had any children.

☐ Child has _____ children.

☐ Child has _____ adopted children.

☐ Child has _____ born children.

	Name of Child at Birth	**Current Name of Child**	**Date of Birth**	**Date of Death**
# 1				
# 2				
# 3				
# 4				
# 5				
# 6				

*****

Name at present: _____

Phone: _____ Fax: _____

Address: _____

_____

Email: _____

Favorite memories:

_____

_____

_____

Name at birth: _____

Place of birth: _____

                                 City   *County*   *State*   *Country*

Child is buried at: _____

Cause of death: _____

☐   Child has never been married.

☐   Child is currently married.

☐   Child has been married _____ times.

	Name of Spouse	Date of Marriage	Date of Divorce	Date of Death
# 1				
# 2				
# 3				

- ☐ Child has not had any children.
- ☐ Child has _____ children.
- ☐ Child has _____ adopted children.
- ☐ Child has _____ born children.

	Name of Child at Birth	Current Name of Child	Date of Birth	Date of Death
# 1				
# 2				
# 3				
# 4				
# 5				
# 6				

*****

Name at present: _____

Phone: _____ Fax: _____

Address: _____

_____

Email: _____

Favorite memories:

_____

_____

_____

Name at birth: _____

Place of birth: _____

                                 City   County   State   Country

Child is buried at: _____

Cause of death: _____

☐ Child has never been married.

☐ Child is currently married.

☐ Child has been married _____ times.

	Name of Spouse	Date of Marriage	Date of Divorce	Date of Death
# 1				
# 2				
# 3				

☐ Child has not had any children.

☐ Child has _____ children.

☐ Child has _____ adopted children.

☐ Child has _____ born children.

	Name of Child at Birth	Current Name of Child	Date of Birth	Date of Death
# 1				
# 2				
# 3				

# 4				
# 5				
# 6				

*****

Name at present: _____

Phone: _____ Fax: _____

Address: _____

_____

Email: _____

Favorite memories: _____

_____

_____

Name at birth: _____

Place of birth: _____

                        City   *Count*   *State*   *Country*

Child is buried at: _____

Cause of death: _____

☐ Child has never been married.

☐ Child is currently married.

☐ Child has been married _____ times.

	Name of Spouse	Date of Marriage	Date of Divorce	Date of Death
# 1				
# 2				
# 3				

☐ Child has not had any children.

☐ Child has _____ children.

☐ Child has _____ adopted children.

☐ Child has _____ born children.

	Name of Child at Birth	Current Name of Child	Date of Birth	Date of Death
# 1				
# 2				
# 3				
# 4				
# 5				
# 6				

Parents

Name: _____

Phone: _____ Fax: _____

Address: _____

_____

Email: _____

Date of Birth: _____ Place of Birth: _____

Date of Death: _____ Cause of Death: _____

Favorite memories:

_____

_____

_____

_____

_____

_____

_____

_____

_____

_____

_____

_____

_____

_____

_____

_____

_____

_____

_____

_____

_____

Name: _____

Phone: _____ Fax: _____

Address: _____

_____

Email: _____

Date of Birth: _____ Place of Birth: _____

Date of Death: _____ Cause of Death: _____

Favorite memories:

_____

_____

_____

_____

_____

_____

_____

_____

_____

_____

_____

_____

_____

_____

_____

_____

_____

_____

_____

_____

_____

_____

_____

_____

Brothers and Sisters

Name at present: _____

Phone: _____ Fax: _____

Address: _____

_____

Email: _____

How this person is related to me: _____

Favorite memories:

_____

_____

_____

_____

Date of birth: _____

Place of birth: _____

City   County   State   Country

Date of death: _____ Cause of death:_____

Sibling is buried at: _____

- ☐ Sibling has never been married.
- ☐ Sibling is currently married.
- ☐ Sibling has been married _____ times.

	Name of Spouse	**Date of Marriage**	**Date of Divorce**	**Date of Death**
# 1				
# 2				
# 3				

- ☐ Sibling has not had any children.
- ☐ Sibling has _____ children.
- ☐ Sibling has _____ adopted children.
- ☐ Sibling has _____ born children.

	Name of Child at Birth	Current Name of Child	Date of Birth	Date of Death
# 1				
# 2				
# 3				
# 4				
# 5				
# 6				

*****

Name at present: _____

Phone: _____ Fax: _____

Address: _____

_____

Email: _____

How this person is related to me: _____

Favorite memories: _____

_____

_____

_____

Date of birth: _____

Place of birth: _____

                      City   County   State   Country

Date of death: _____ Cause of death: _____

Sibling is buried at: _____

- ☐ Sibling has never been married.
- ☐ Sibling is currently married.
- ☐ Sibling has been married _____ times.

	Name of Spouse	Date of Marriage	Date of Divorce	Date of Death
# 1				
# 2				
# 3				

- ☐ Sibling has not had any children.
- ☐ Sibling has _____ children.
- ☐ Sibling has _____ adopted children.
- ☐ Sibling has _____ born children.

	Name of Child at Birth	Current Name of Child	Date of Birth	Date of Death
# 1				
# 2				
# 3				
# 4				
# 5				
# 6				

*****

Name at present: _____

Phone: _____ Fax: _____

Address: _____

_____

Email: _____

How this person is related to me: _____

Favorite memories:

_____

_____

_____

_____

Date of birth: _____

Place of birth: _____

                                    City   County   State   Country

Date of death: _____ Cause of death:_____

Sibling is buried at: _____

☐ Sibling has never been married.

☐ Sibling is currently married.

☐ Sibling has been married _____ times.

	Name of Spouse	Date of Marriage	Date of Divorce	Date of Death
# 1				
# 2				
# 3				

☐ Sibling has not had any children.

☐ Sibling has _____ children.

☐ Sibling has _____ adopted children.

☐ Sibling has _____ born children.

	Name of Child at Birth	Current Name of Child	Date of Birth	Date of Death
# 1				
# 2				
# 3				

# 4				
# 5				
# 6				

*****

Name at present: _____

Phone: _____ Fax: _____

Address: _____

_____

Email: _____

How this person is related to me: _____

Favorite memories:

_____

_____

_____

Date of birth: _____

Place of birth: _____

City   County   State   Country

Date of death: _____ Cause of death: _____

Sibling is buried at: _____

☐ Sibling has never been married.

☐ Sibling is currently married.

☐ Sibling has been married _____ times.

	Name of Spouse	Date of Marriage	Date of Divorce	Date of Death
# 1				
# 2				
# 3				

☐ Sibling has not had any children.

☐ Sibling has _____ children.

☐ Sibling has _____ adopted children.

☐ Sibling has _____ born children.

	Name of Child at Birth	Current Name of Child	Date of Birth	Date of Death
# 1				
# 2				
# 3				
# 4				
# 5				
# 6				

*****

Name at present: _____

Phone: _____ Fax: _____

Address: _____

_____

Email: _____

How this person is related to me: _____

Favorite memories:

_____

_____

_____

_____

Date of birth: _____

Place of birth: _____

       City   County   State   Country

Date of death: _____ Cause of death: _____

Sibling is buried at _____

- ☐ Sibling has never been married.
- ☐ Sibling is currently married.
- ☐ Sibling has been married _____ times.

	Name of Spouse	Date of Marriage	Date of Divorce	Date of Death
# 1				
# 2				
# 3				

- ☐ Sibling has not had any children.
- ☐ Sibling has _____ children.
- ☐ Sibling has _____ adopted children.
- ☐ Sibling has _____ born children.

	Name of Child at Birth	Current Name of Child	Date of Birth	Date of Death
# 1				
# 2				
# 3				
# 4				
# 5				
# 6				

*****

Name at present: _____

Phone: _____ Fax: _____

Address: _____

_____

Email: _____

How this person is related to me: _____

Favorite memories:

_____

_____

_____

_____

Date of birth: _____

Place of birth: _____

                        City   *County*   *State*   *Country*

Date of death: _____ Cause of death: _____

Sibling is buried at: _____

- ☐ Sibling has never been married.
- ☐ Sibling is currently married.
- ☐ Sibling has been married _____ times.

	Name of Spouse	Date of Marriage	Date of Divorce	Date of Death
# 1				
# 2				
# 3				

- ☐ Sibling has not had any children.
- ☐ Sibling has _____ children.
- ☐ Sibling has _____ adopted children.
- ☐ Sibling has _____ born children.

	Name of Child at Birth	Current Name of Child	Date of Birth	Date of Death
# 1				
# 2				
# 3				
# 4				
# 5				
# 6				

Grandparents

Name: _____

Relationship: _____

Phone: _____ Fax: _____

Address: _____

_____

Email: _____

Date of Birth: _____ Place of Birth: _____

Date of Death: _____ Cause of Death: _____

Favorite memories:

_____

_____

_____

_____

_____

Name: _____

Relationship: _____

Phone: _____ Fax: _____

Address: _____

_____

Email: _____

Date of Birth: _____ Place of Birth: _____

Date of Death: _____ Cause of Death: _____

Favorite memories:

_____

_____

_____

_____

_____

Name: _____

Relationship: _____

Phone: _____ Fax: _____

Address: _____

_____

Email: _____

Date of Birth: _____ Place of Birth: _____

Date of Death: _____ Cause of Death: _____

Favorite memories:

_____

_____

_____

_____

_____

Name: _____

Relationship: _____

Phone: _____ Fax: _____

Address: _____

_____

Email: _____

Date of Birth: _____ Place of Birth: _____

Date of Death: _____ Cause of Death: _____

Favorite memories:

_____

_____

_____

_____

_____

Aunts, Uncles, and Cousins

Name: _____

Phone: _____ Fax: _____

Address: _____

_____

Email: _____

How this person is related to me: _____

Date of Birth: _____ Place of Birth: _____

Date of Death:_____ Cause of Death: _____

Favorite memories:

_____

_____

_____

_____

_____

Name: _____

Phone: _____ Fax: _____

Address: _____

_____

Email: _____

How this person is related to me: _____

Date of Birth: _____ Place of Birth: _____

Date of Death:_____ Cause of Death: _____

Favorite memories:

_____

_____

_____

_____

_____

Name: _____

Phone: _____ Fax: _____

Address: _____

_____

Email: _____

How this person is related to me: _____

Date of Birth: _____ Place of Birth: _____

Date of Death: _____ Cause of Death: _____

Favorite memories:

_____

_____

_____

_____

_____

Name: _____

Phone: _____ Fax: _____

Address: _____

_____

Email: _____

How this person is related to me: _____

Date of Birth: _____ Place of Birth: _____

Date of Death: _____ Cause of Death: _____

Favorite memories:

_____

_____

_____

_____

_____

Name: _____

Phone: _____ Fax: _____

Address: _____

_____

Email: _____

How this person is related to me: _____

Date of Birth: _____ Place of Birth: _____

Date of Death: _____ Cause of Death: _____

Favorite memories:

_____

_____

_____

_____

_____

Name: _____

Phone: _____ Fax: _____

Address: _____

_____

Email: _____

How this person is related to me: _____

Date of Birth: _____ Place of Birth: _____

Date of Death: _____ Cause of Death: _____

Favorite memories:

_____

_____

_____

_____

_____

Stepparents

Name: _____

Relationship: _____

Phone: _____ Fax: _____

Address: _____

_____

Date of Birth: _____ Place of Birth: _____

Date of Death: _____ Cause of Death: _____

Email: _____

Favorite memories:

_____

_____

_____

_____

_____

_____

Name: _____

Relationship: _____

Phone: _____ Fax: _____

Address: _____

_____

Email: _____

Date of Birth: _____ Place of Birth: _____

Date of Death: _____ Cause of Death: _____

Favorite memories:

_____

_____

_____

_____

_____

Stepbrothers and sisters

Name: _____

Relationship: _____

Phone: _____ Fax: _____

Address: _____

_____

Email: _____

Date of Birth: _____ Place of Birth: _____

Date of Death: _____ Cause of Death: _____

Favorite memories:

_____

_____

_____

_____

_____

Name: _____

Relationship: _____

Phone: _____ Fax: _____

Address: _____

_____

Email: _____

Favorite memories:

_____

_____

_____

_____

_____

Name: _____

Relationship: _____

Phone: _____ Fax: _____

Address: _____

_____

Email: _____

Date of Birth: _____ Place of Birth: _____

Date of Death: _____ Cause of Death: _____

Favorite memories:

_____

_____

_____

_____

_____

Name: _____

Relationship: _____

Phone: _____ Fax: _____

Address: _____

_____

Email: _____

Date of Birth: _____ Place of Birth: _____

Date of Death: _____ Cause of Death: _____

Favorite memories:

_____

_____

_____

_____

_____

Family Medical History

The following documents explain my family medical history. I or any of my blood relatives (including parents, grandparents, sisters, brothers, uncles, aunts, and children) have had the following:

Yes   **Who**

☐   Alcoholism   _____

☐   Allergies   _____

☐   Alzheimer's disease   _____

☐   Arthritis   _____

☐   Asthma   _____

☐   Birth defects   _____

☐   Blood disorder   _____

☐   Cancer   _____

☐   Chromosomal disorder   _____

☐   Cystic fibrosis   _____

☐   Diabetes   _____

☐   Dementia   _____

☐   Endometriosis   _____

☐   Eczema   _____

☐   Epilepsy   _____

☐   Gallbladder problems   _____

☐   Glaucoma   _____

☐   Gout   _____

☐   Hay fever   _____

☐   Hearing loss   _____

☐   Heart disease   _____

☐   High blood pressure   _____

☐   High cholesterol   _____

☐   Inflammatory bowel disease   _____

☐   Infertility   _____

☐   Kidney disease   _____

☐   Learning disabilities   _____

☐   Lung disease   _____

☐   Lymphoma   _____

☐   Mental disorder   _____

☐   Mental retardation   _____

☐   Miscarriage, stillbirth   _____

☐   Muscular dystrophy   _____

☐   Neurological disorders   _____

☐   Osteoporosis   _____

☐   Psoriasis   _____

☐   Sickle cell disease   _____

☐   Stomach disorders   _____

☐   Stroke   _____

☐   Thyroid disorder   _____

☐   Ulcers   _____

☐   Vision Impairment   _____

☐   Other   _____

☐   Other   _____

Family History: Other

The following miscellaneous information about my family history may be of interest to my heirs:

_____

_____

_____

_____

_____

_____

_____

_____

_____

_____

_____

_____

_____

_____

_____

_____

_____

_____

_____

_____

_____

_____

_____

_____

_____

_____

_____

_____

_____

_____

CHAPTER 3
INSURANCE

If you can keep your head when all about you
Are loving theirs and blaming it on you...
If you can meet with Triumph and Disaster
And threat those two imposters the same...
Yours is the Earth and everything that's in it,
And – which is more—you'll be a Man, my son!

—Rudyard Kipling

Insurance offers a way to spread the risk of financial loss among many people. The payment of annual premiums protects the insured (to the limits of the policy) against losses from fire, theft, accident, or liability, depending on the type of insurance purchased. Any loss is shared by all of those insured, saving the individual from financial disaster. The group, in other words, absorbs the individual's unexpected losses.

If something happens to you—death, an accident, a stroke, or other event that prevents you from continuing to conduct your own business affairs—your loved ones may have to file insurance claims, cancel certain policies, or obtain new ones in order to protect your property. To be able to take advantage of the insurance that you have obtained to protect your family and property, your family needs to know about all your insurance policies. An amazing number of insurance proceeds go unclaimed because the policyholder's family or heirs were never told about them. Use the checklists in this chapter so your family has a record of your various policies with the names and addresses of the agents and companies.

My Checklist

Done   **Need to Do**

☐   ☐   Review terms of all insurance policies

☐   ☐   Locate all insurance policies

☐   ☐   Review the beneficiaries on any life insurance policy

☐   ☐   Annually review your health insurance options

☐   ☐   Complete the checklists for Chapter 3

Insurance Checklists

The checklists in Chapter 3 are set out in the following order:

- *Annuity*
- *Automobile Insurance*
- *Health Insurance: Disability, Medicare, and Long-Term Care*
- *Homeowners Insurance*
- *Life Insurance*
- *Other Residence Insurance*
- *Umbrella Policy Insurance*
- *Vehicle Insurance*
- *Insurance: Other*

The following descriptions are not a detailed breakdown of the many types of insurance options available. They should, however, give you some information about the most widely used types of insurance coverage to help you organize your own policies.

Annuity

Annuities are a type of insurance that are typically designed to provide a stream of income. As with other types of insurance, there are many types of annuities. They may be fixed, variable, or indexed—depending on how your principal is invested, with immediate or deferred payments—depending on when you need payouts. Typically, money invested in the annuity grows tax-deferred, with payouts being taxed when received as return of principal and ordinary income.

You can have many options as to how your money is invested within the annuity, at what point your annuity begins to make payments, and for how long and to whom payments will be made. Payouts may be made for a fixed number of years, or during your lifetime, or for the lifetime of a spouse or other beneficiary. At additional cost you can also obtain specific benefits, such as a guaranteed minimum death benefit, or a guaranteed minimum withdrawal benefit. A guaranteed minimum death benefit, or GMDB rider, means that your beneficiaries or your estate will receive a set amount as defined in the contract if you die before the annuity begins paying benefits. A guaranteed minimum withdrawal benefit, or GMWB, means that while you are alive you will receive a fixed percentage of your investment each year. Be certain you understand the terms of any annuity you have and periodically review your annuity contact to confirm that it continues to fit your needs.

Life Insurance

Life insurance is primarily intended to ease the financial loss to a beneficiary that results from the policyholder's death. Although death comes to everyone and cannot be considered "unexpected" in the long run, it can certainly be unexpected when it occurs. Life insurance is a way to make sure that your family has cash to pay for your final expenses, such as for your funeral or the expenses of your final illness. You may also want to consider if you want to have an insurance policy that would provide cash for any estate taxes or unpaid debts. Life insurance also may be important to provide financial support to your spouse or dependent children after your death.

✔ Review terms of all life insurance policies

Today's life insurance market has multiple options for you to choose from including how much coverage you purchase, the size of the premiums, how the policy is invested, any guarantees on returns, and how and when the policy proceeds are paid out to your beneficiaries. Before purchasing any policy you need to be certain you understand all of the options and the risks involved. Do your homework to compare your options with multiple insurance companies. Also seek competent advice on any tax consequences to you and your estate that the various options can have.

A life insurance policy pays a designated sum of money to the person you name as your beneficiary upon your death. Your beneficiary can be your estate or one or more individuals. Be sure you understand the possible tax consequences when making this decision. This money may be paid in a lump sum, in a monthly sum for the life of another individual, in monthly sums over a certain length of time, or in some other manner spelled out by the terms of your policy. Regardless of what payment method you select, the amount your beneficiary will receive is set out in the policy. It may even pay double if your death is caused by accident—a so-called *double indemnity* policy.

A widely purchased form of life insurance is *whole life insurance*. This type of insurance pays a sum of money (the "face value") to your beneficiary at the time of your death. You will have paid a premium each year to keep the insurance in force. The amount of the premium is determined by your age at the time you purchased the policy. The younger you are, the smaller the premium on the policy. Variations in the method of payment for whole life insurance are available. For example, you might obtain a policy which requires annual premiums for 20 years. At the expiration of the 20-year period, the policy continues in effect for the balance of your life, but you do not have to continue paying the premiums. It is even possible for you to purchase a policy by making one large initial premium payment. Regardless of payment, whole life insurance provides coverage for the rest of your life (as long as you have paid all the required premiums).

Universal Life, variable whole life and variable universal life are different types of permanent life insurance in which you have the option to vary (within the terms of the contract) the amount you pay in premiums from year to year and how your policy's cash reserves grow. Typically the cash value reserves held by the insurance company are invested in stocks, bonds, or mutual funds. You, as the policy holder, are able to select the investment from a menu offered by the insurance company. Some policies have guaranteed minimum returns on the investment; others allow you to borrow against the cash value during your life. How much your beneficiary would receive at your death varies based on many factors depending on the terms of the policy, the amounts paid in premiums, and the investment success of the insurance company.

Term insurance, on the other hand, provides insurance coverage only for a specified length of time. You might purchase a policy that provides coverage for 5 years, 10 years, or 20 years. The annual premium for term insurance is substantially less than the annual premium for whole life insurance. The cost of purchasing the same amount of coverage gradually increases with the age of the purchaser. Many term life insurance contracts provide that the policy may be renewed at the end of the term without providing further proof of insurability. The premium for the renewed term will most likely be higher than for the original term because you would be older. Other term policies provide that they may be converted, within a certain period, into a permanent type of life or endowment insurance without proof of insurability. Once again, the premium would be adjusted.

✔ Locate all insurance policies

Regardless of the type of life insurance you hold, it is important that your life insurance policies be readily available at death, that they be kept in a safe place, and that your heirs know where they are located. Some companies may require that your heirs hand over your original life insurance policies before they can collect any proceeds.

Many employers provide life insurance for their employees, and partnerships often fund buy-sell agreements with life insurance. Be sure to include information about work-related insurance in the checklists in this chapter. You don't want your heirs to overlook any policies.

✔ **Review the beneficiaries you have listed on your policies**

Now is a good time to review each policy to make sure you have properly listed the beneficiaries you want to receive the policy proceeds. Circumstances may have changed since you initially named the beneficiaries on your policies. For example, you probably don't want to have a former spouse as a beneficiary (unless you are required to maintain a policy under a divorce decree). Your family may have changed with marriages, divorces, births of children and grandchildren, and deaths. A beneficiary you named several years ago may now be deceased. It's a good idea to name successor or secondary beneficiaries in case a primary beneficiary dies before you do.

✔ **Annually review your health insurance options**

Health Insurance

Health insurance provides a means to pay doctor, hospital and other medical expenses if you become sick or are in an accident. Most people get health insurance as an employee benefit where they work. Some people can continue to get health coverage through their former employer's health plan after they retire. Employers don't have to provide *retiree health insurance* and they can cut or eliminate those benefits. Before you retire, or if you are retired, be sure you know what health benefits are available to you. Get this information from your employer's benefit coordinator. Typically, with group health insurance you have an opportunity each year to modify your coverage.

Many different types of accident and illness insurance policies exist. Some are very limited in scope and pay out only if you develop a specific type of illness, such as cancer. Other policies, however, provide very broad coverage, though each has its limitations. Before purchasing any type of health insurance be certain you understand what is and is not covered.

Medical expense reimbursement policies range from a policy that pays $10 for each day you are hospitalized to health insurance policies that cover almost every medical expense that the policyholder could incur. Because the coverage varies to such a great extent, the cost of medical and accident coverage varies greatly.

Medicare

Medicare is a federal health insurance program for people who are age 65 and over, for some younger people with disabilities, and for people with end-stage kidney disease. The Medicare program has several parts. *Part A* helps pay for inpatient hospital care, as well as some home health care, preventive screenings, hospice care, and skilled nursing care. You do not have to pay any premiums for Part A coverage because you have already paid for it through your payroll taxes.

Part B helps pay for doctor visits, some home health care, medical equipment, some preventive services, outpatient hospital care, rehabilitative therapy, laboratory text, X-rays, mental health services, ambulance services, and blood transfusions. When you turn age 65 you are automatically signed up for Part A and Part B if you are receiving Social Security or Railroad Retirement benefits. You do have to pay premiums for Part B. Depending on your circumstances, you will pay $96.40, $110.50, or $115.40 in 2011. If your capable income is over $85,000 for an individual or $170,000 for a married couple filing jointly your premiums will be between $161.50 and $369.10. You can decline Part B if you are covered by another policy. You can later sign up for Part B if your employer or retiree coverage ends, but you have only a short time to apply for Part B. If you wait too long, you will have to pay more in premiums.

Part C is now known as Medicare Advantage. Medicare Advantage plans are offered by private companies. You have the option of purchasing Medicare Advantage coverage. These policies pay for the same services as Parts A and B and may offer other benefits such as dental, vision, and drug coverage. In most Medicare Advantage plans you can only go to doctors, specialists, and hospitals that are on the plan's list of providers. During open enrollment periods between October and December of each year you can change Medicare Advantage plans or select original Medicare (Part A and Part B).

Part D helps pay for prescription drugs. You have the option of purchasing prescription drug coverage through private insurance companies that have been approved by Medicare to sell this type of insurance. You can choose from many drug plans offered by many companies. The benefits and costs vary among insurance companies and each company's several plans. You can elect to purchase Part D drug coverage when you are newly eligible for Medicare; if you wait you will have to pay a late enrollment penalty. Each year you can switch plans during a fall open enrollment period.

Medicare doesn't pay for all health care costs. You are responsible for an annual deductible, coinsurance or co-payments. Medicare also does not pay for long-term care. You may want to consider purchasing Medicare supplemental insurance, also called ***Medigap*** insurance. Medigap insurance covers some of the costs that Medicare does not pay. This private health insurance is offered by Medicare-approved insurance companies that can offer up to 11 standardized plans. These standard plans are labeled Plans A through G and K through N. Each standard plan offers a different set of benefits, fills different gaps in Medicare coverage, and varies in price. This means that the benefits covered in one company's "Plan B" would be the same as those covered by another company, but the prices the companies charge can be different. The standardization of plans helps you more easily compare policies among companies.

You can compare the various Medicare plans, including prescription drug, Medigap and Medicare Advantage, at www.medicare.gov/find-a-plan.

Automobile Insurance

Automobile insurance is pretty much a necessity for any owner of a motor vehicle. In fact, many states require all drivers to be insured for liability to other persons for damages resulting from an automobile accident. Regardless of the law in your particular state, it makes good sense to insure yourself against the claims by others and against any expenses that you might have you have a collision or fire, or your car or truck is stolen. You also should have insurance for motorcycles, motorboats, snowmobiles, and other recreational vehicles that you own.

Homeowners Insurance

Originally, fire insurance was about the only type of insurance that a homeowner could obtain on his or her residence. As the various insurance lines developed, insurance became available to protect against windstorm, hail, flood, explosion, riot, smoke damage, etc. Insurance is now also available for the contents of your home, as well as your garage or any outbuildings.

Today, most homeowners purchase a homeowners policy that combines fire and extended insurance coverage that also includes protection for your personal property, additional living expenses if you can't live in your home because of damage, and comprehensive personal liability coverage. This liability coverage would make medical payments to guests who get injured in your home and pay for some damage to the property of others. Rather than having to purchase separate policies to cover each of these various risks, the homeowners policy combines them into one policy. Similar types of policies are available to condominium owners and renters. You can also add *riders* to your policy to fit specific needs, or to insure special items such as antiques or jewelry.

Other Insurance

Many insurance companies offer additional insurance liability protection through an *umbrella policy,* which provides insurance coverage in excess of your regular automobile, personal liability, and other liability coverage. It is usually sold in multiples of $1 million and is a low-cost method of buying substantial protection.

Heirs Checklist

✔ Immediately contact the insurance agent to ensure that the home and its contents are properly insured during the administration of the estate.

✔ Make sure that a homeowners policy remains in effect if no one is going to be living in the residence during an extended nursing home stay or following the death of the homeowner.

✔ Contact the insurance company for instructions on how to file a claim for life insurance benefits.

✔ Notify the vehicle insurance company so there will complete coverage until the vehicle is sold or transferred to its next owner.

CHAPTER 3
INSURANCE CHECKLISTS

Annuity

☐   I do not have an annuity.

☐   I have an annuity with the following policies and companies:

Insurance company: _____

Agent: _____

Phone: _____ Fax: _____

Address: _____

_____

Email: _____ Website: _____

Policy #: _____

Terms: _____

Beneficiary/beneficiaries: _____

Insurance company: _____

Agent: _____

Phone: _____ Fax: _____

Address: _____

_____

Email: _____ Website: _____

Policy #: _____

Terms: _____

Beneficiary/beneficiaries: _____

Automobile Insurance

I carry automobile insurance on the following vehicles with the following companies:

Vehicle: _____

Year purchased: _____ Purchase price: _____

Insurance company: _____

Agent: _____

Phone: _____ Fax: _____

Address: _____

_____

Email: _____ Website: _____

Policy #: _____

Vehicle: _____

Year purchased: _____ Purchase price: _____

Insurance company: _____

Agent: _____

Phone: _____ Fax: _____

Address: _____

_____

Email: _____ Website: _____

Policy #: _____

Vehicle: _____

Year purchased: _____ Purchase price: _____

Insurance company: _____

Agent: _____

Phone: _____ Fax: _____

Address: _____

_____

Email: _____ Website: _____

Policy #: _____

Vehicle: _____

Year purchased: _____ Purchase price: _____

Insurance company: _____

Agent: _____

Phone: _____ Fax: _____

Address: _____

_____

Email: _____ Website: _____

Policy #: _____

Health Insurance: Disability, Medicare, and Long-Term Care

☐ I do not carry health insurance.

☐ I carry health insurance with the following policies and companies:

  ☐ Dental

  ☐ Disability

  ☐ Hospitalization

  ☐ Long-term care

  ☐ Major medical

  ☐ Medicare

  ☐ Medicare Advantage

  ☐ Medicare Supplemental Insurance (Medigap)

  ☐ Medicare Part D Prescription Drug Insurance

  ☐ Surgical

  ☐ Travel accidental death

  ☐ Vision

  ☐ Other

Insurance company: _____

Type of policy: _____

Agent: _____

Phone: _____ Fax: _____

Address: _____

_____

Email: _____ Website: _____

Policy #: _____

Group #: _____

Policy due date: _____

Insurance company: _____

Type of policy: _____

Agent: _____

Phone: _____ Fax: _____

Address: _____

_____

Email: _____ Website: _____

Policy #: _____

Group #: _____

Policy due date:_____

Insurance company: _____

Type of policy: _____

Agent: _____

Phone: _____ Fax: _____

Address: _____

_____

Email: _____ Website: _____

Policy #: _____

Group #: _____

Policy due date:_____

Insurance company: _____

Type of policy: _____

Agent: _____

Phone: _____ Fax: _____

Address: _____

_____

Email: _____ Website: _____

Policy #: _____

Group #: _____

Policy due date:_____

Insurance company: _____

Type of policy: _____

Agent: _____

Phone: _____ Fax: _____

Address: _____

_____

Email: _____ Website: _____

Policy #: _____

Group #: _____

Policy due date:_____

Insurance company: _____

Type of policy: _____

Agent: _____

Phone: _____ Fax: _____

Address: _____

_____

Email: _____ Website: _____

Policy #: _____

Group #: _____

Policy due date:_____

Homeowners Insurance

- ☐ I do not carry homeowners or residence insurance.
- ☐ I carry homeowners or residence insurance with the following policies and companies:

Insurance company: _____

Agent: _____

Phone: _____ Fax: _____

Address: _____

_____

Email: _____ Website: _____

Policy #: _____

Description of coverage:

_____

_____

Insurance company: _____

Agent: _____

Phone: _____ Fax: _____

Address: _____

_____

Email: _____ Website: _____

Policy #: _____

Description of coverage:

_____

_____

Life Insurance

□   I do not carry life insurance.

□   I carry life insurance with the following policies and companies:

Insurance company: _____

Agent: _____

Phone: _____ Fax: _____

Address: _____

_____

Email: _____ Website: _____

Policy #: _____

Face amount: _____

Beneficiary/beneficiaries: _____

Insurance company: _____

Agent: _____

Phone: _____ Fax: _____

Address: _____

_____

Email: _____ Website: _____

Policy #: _____

Face amount: _____

Beneficiary/beneficiaries: _____

Other Residence Insurance

☐ I do not carry insurance for another residence, apartment, or condominium.

☐ I carry homeowners, renters, or condominium, or residence insurance with the following policies and companies:

Insurance company: _____

Residence location: _____

Agent: _____

Phone: _____ Fax: _____

Address: _____

_____

Email: _____ Website: _____

Policy #: _____

Description of coverage: _____

_____

Insurance company: _____

Residence location: _____

Agent: _____

Phone: _____ Fax: _____

Address: _____

_____

Email: _____ Website: _____

Policy #: _____

Description of coverage: _____

_____

Umbrella Policy Insurance

☐ I do not carry umbrella policy insurance.

☐ I carry umbrella policy insurance with the following policies and companies:

Insurance company: _____

Agent: _____

Phone: _____ Fax: _____

Address: _____

_____

Email: _____ Website: _____

Policy #: _____

Group #: _____

Type of policy: _____

Policy due date: _____

Insurance company: _____

Agent: _____

Phone: _____ Fax: _____

Address: _____

_____

Email: _____ Website: _____

Policy #: _____

Group #: _____

Type of policy: _____

Policy due date: _____

Vehicle Insurance

I carry vehicle insurance on the following vehicles (airplanes, boats, motorcycles, snowmobiles, etc.) with the following companies:

Vehicle: _____

Year purchased: _____ Purchase price: _____

Insurance company: _____

Agent: _____

Phone: _____ Fax: _____

Address: _____

_____

Email: _____ Website: _____

Policy #: _____

Vehicle: _____

Year purchased: _____ Purchase price: _____

Insurance company: _____

Agent: _____

Phone: _____ Fax: _____

Address: _____

_____

Email: _____ Website: _____

Policy #: _____

Vehicle: _____

Year purchased: _____ Purchase price: _____

Insurance company: _____

Agent: _____

Phone: _____ Fax: _____

Address: _____

_____

Email: _____ Website: _____

Policy #: _____

Insurance: Other

The following miscellaneous information about my insurance may be of interest to my heirs:

_____

_____

_____

_____

_____

_____

_____

_____

_____

_____

_____

_____

_____

_____

_____

_____

_____

_____

_____

_____

_____

_____

_____

_____

_____

CHAPTER 4
BENEFITS FOR SURVIVORS

There are only two ways to live your life. One is as though nothing is a miracle. The other is as though everything is a miracle.

—Albert Einstein

Most of us are aware of retirement benefits from Social Security, disability benefits for military veterans, worker's disability compensation for job-related injuries and illness, and retirement payments from private and public pension plans. But you may be unaware of the benefits from the same sources that can help your survivors. This chapter is primarily concerned with benefits that may be available to your survivors.

My Checklist

Done	Need to Do	
☐	☐	Apply for Social Security benefits
☐	☐	Apply for veterans benefits
☐	☐	Get a copy of military service record
☐	☐	Apply for workers' compensation
☐	☐	Identify all available pension benefits
☐	☐	Manage disbursements from your retirement plans
☐	☐	Verify the beneficiary designation on pension or retirement plans
☐	☐	Complete the checklists for Chapter 4

Benefits for Survivors Checklists

The checklists in Chapter 4 are set out in the following order:

- *Pensions*
- *Retirement Plans*
- *Social Security Benefits*
- *Veterans Benefits*
- *Workers' Compensation*
- *Benefits: Other*

✔ Apply for Social Security benefits

Social Security Benefits

Social Security can be an important source of continuing income when your family's earnings are reduced or stopped because of your retirement, disability, or death.

Before you or your family can receive monthly cash benefits, you must be credited for a certain amount of work under Social Security. For most benefits you must have at least ten years of Social Security-covered employment. Just how many credits you must establish depends on your age and whether you or your family is applying for retirement, survivor, or disability benefits. You can find details on specific requirements at www.ssa.gov or at any Social Security Administration (SSA) office located throughout the country. You can find those addresses at the SSA website or in the blue pages of your phone book.

You can start receiving retirement checks as early as age 62 and disability checks at any age. However, you will get up to a 30 percent reduction if you start receiving retirement benefits before your full retirement age. If you were born between 1943 and 1954 your full retirement age is 66. If you wait until age 70 to take Social Security retirement benefits you get an additional amount, but, of course, you will receive those payments for fewer years. Check out the chart at www.ssa.gov/pubs/ageincrease.htm for more details on how your benefit amount changes based on when you start taking benefits.

If you are receiving retirement benefits, or in some cases just eligible to receive benefits, or receiving disability benefits, your family members are also eligible for benefits under the following circumstances:

- Unmarried children under 18 (or 19 if a full-time elementary or secondary school student);
- Unmarried children 18 or over who were severely disabled before age 22, and who continue to be disabled;

- A wife or husband 62 or older who has been married to the worker for at least one year; or
- A wife or husband under 62 if she or he is caring for a child under 16 (or disabled) who is receiving a benefit under the worker's earnings.

A divorced spouse who has been divorced at least two years can receive benefits at age 62 regardless of whether the former spouse receives them. The marriage must have lasted ten years or more; the former spouse must be at least 62 and eligible for Social Security benefits, regardless of whether he or she has retired; and the divorced spouse must not be eligible for an equal or higher benefit on his or her own—or anyone else's—Social Security record.

Survivor Benefits: Your heirs should be aware of benefits that may be available after your death. There are a number of benefits available to your surviving family members.

- Your spouse and minor children may be entitled to a one-time $255 lump sum payment.

Social Security survivors insurance can provide cash benefits based on your earnings record to the following:

- Your spouse can get full benefits at full retirement age, or reduced benefits as early as age 60;
- Your disabled spouse is eligible for benefits as early as age 50;
- Your spouse at any age if he or she takes care of your child who is under age 16 or disabled, and receiving Social Security benefits;
- Your unmarried children under 18, or up to age 19 if they are attending high school full time. Under certain circumstances, benefits can be paid to stepchildren, grandchildren, or adopted children;
- Your children at any age who were disabled before age 22 and remain disabled;
- Your dependent parents who are age 62 or older.

Medicare, federal hospital and medical insurance, is available to help protect you from the high costs of health care when you are 65 or older. You or your spouse must have worked for at least ten years in Medicare-covered employment. Disabled individuals under age 65 are also eligible for Medicare after they have been entitled to Social Security disability benefits for 24 or more months. Insured workers and their dependents who need dialysis treatment or a kidney transplant because of permanent kidney failure also have Medicare protection at any age.

Medicare benefits are only available to you. There is no family coverage for spouses or dependents. Your spouse will be eligible for Medicare at age 65 even if he or she does not have enough years of covered employment.

You should apply for your Medicare insurance at least three months before your 65th birthday so your protection can start at age 65. If you are on Social Security when you reach age 65 you will automatically be enrolled in Medicare.

Applying for Social Security benefits

You should begin your application for Social Security retirement benefits about three months before the month you want to start receiving your benefit. You can apply online at www.socialsecurity.gov/info/isba/retirement/ or by going to your local Social Security office. When you apply for Social Security benefits, you should have original documents or certified copies of the following with you:

✔ Your own Social Security card or a record of your number;

✔ Proof of your age (a birth certificate or baptismal certificate made within five years after your birth).

Have this information available for your heirs so they can more easily apply for the benefits they are entitled to receive.

Note: Because the Social Security Act is amended from time to time, this may not be the latest information concerning benefits to which you or your heirs may be entitled. Contact the nearest Social Security Administration office for a full explanation of your rights under the law.

✔ Apply for veterans benefits

Veterans benefits

The Department of Veterans Affairs (VA) is charged with administering benefits available to persons who have served on active duty in the U.S. military service. The available benefits depend upon the veteran's length of service, the era during which the service was performed, whether the veteran is disabled, whether the disability was caused by active service, and many other criteria.

✔ Get a copy of military service record

You and your family will need to have documentation of your military service to apply for any benefits available to you or to your family. You can get a copy of your service record (DD 214) at www.archives.gov/veterans/military-service-records/get-service-records.html.

Under certain circumstances, the following benefits (and many more) *may* be available to you if you are a veteran:

• Pensions for disability caused by service-connected injury or disease

• Pensions for certain non-service-connected disabilities

- Automobile allowance for service-connected loss, or permanent loss of the use of one or both hands or feet
- Hospitalization benefits
- Alcohol and drug dependence treatment
- Nursing home care
- Outpatient medical treatment
- Prosthetic appliances
- Vocational rehabilitation and counseling
- Loan guaranty benefits
- Insurance
- Federal civil service preference

Many other services and benefits are available to your family if you are an eligible veteran. Certain of these benefits are available to your survivors if you were separated from the service under conditions other than dishonorable.

Burial flag. An American flag may be issued to drape over your casket if you are an eligible veteran. After the funeral service, the flag may be given to your next of kin or close friend or associate. Flags are issued at any VA office and most local post offices. A Presidential Memorial Certificate is also available at no cost to your family.

Burial in national cemeteries. Burial in a national cemetery is open to all members of the Armed Forces and veterans having met minimum active service duty requirements and having been discharged under conditions other than dishonorable. Your spouse, widow or widower, minor children and, under certain conditions, unmarried adult children, are also eligible for burial in a national cemetery. Eligible spouses may be buried in a national cemetary, even if he or she predeceases you. In most cases, one gravesite is provided for the burial of all eligible family members and a single headstone or marker is provided. When both you and your spouse are veterans, you can request two gravesites and two headstones or markers. Certain members of the Armed Forces reserve components may also be eligible for burial. In each instance, space must be available. There is no charge for the grave plot, for its opening and closing, a grave liner, or for perpetual care.

Headstones or markers. The VA will furnish a government headstone or marker to be placed at your grave at any cemetery around the world. Even if the grave was previously marked, your family can obtain a government headstone. This service is provided for eligible veterans whether they are buried in a national cemetery or elsewhere. A headstone or marker is automatically furnished if burial is in a national cemetery. Otherwise, your family must apply to the VA. The VA will ship the headstone or marker, without charge, to the person or firm designated on the application. The VA will also furnish a medallion, on request, to place on an existing headstone or marker that indicates that the person was a veteran. Your family must pay the cost of setting the headstone or marker, or attaching the medallion.

Military Honors. By law every eligible veteran may receive a military funeral honors ceremony, to include folding and presenting the United States burial flag and the playing of Taps. A military funeral honors detail consists of two or more uniformed military persons, with at least one being a member of your branch of the armed forces. The Department of Defense program, "Honoring Those Who Served," calls for funeral directors to request military funeral honors on behalf of your family. Veterans' organizations may assist in providing military funeral honors. In support of this program, VA national cemetery staff can help coordinate military funeral honors either at a national or private cemetery. For more information go to www.militaryfuneralhonors.osd.mil/

Reimbursement of burial expenses. The VA is authorized to pay an allowance toward your funeral and burial expenses if you are an eligible veteran. If it was a service-related death, the VA will pay up to $2,000 toward burial expenses. If you are to be buried in a VA national cemetery, some or all of the cost of transporting your body to the cemetery may be reimbursed. For a nonservice-related death, the VA will pay up to $300 toward burial and funeral expenses and a $300 plot-interment allowance. If your death happens while you are in a VA hospital or under VA contracted nursing home care, some or all of the costs for transporting your remains may be reimbursed.

Dependency and Indemnity Compensation (DIC). DIC payments may be authorized for your spouse, unmarried children, and low-income parents if you die during active duty, or if your death is service-connected. The amount of the basic benefit is determined by your military pay grade. Payments are also made for children under age 18 or up to age 23 who are attending school.

Nonservice connected death pension. Your surviving spouse and unmarried children under age 18 or up to age 23 who are attending school may be eligible for a pension if their income does not exceed certain limits.

Education for spouses, widows, widowers, sons, and daughters. If you are completely disabled or die as a result of your military service, the VA will generally (but with some exceptions) pay to help educate your spouse, widow or widower, and each son and daughter beyond the secondary school level, including college, graduate school, technical and vocational schools, apprenticeships, and on-the-job training programs. Education loans are also available.

Your heirs can get assistance in applying for available benefits through the Department of Veterans Affairs. For comprehensive information about veterans benefits, request a copy of the *Federal Benefits Manual for Veterans and Dependents* from your local VA office. Survivors can also contact the Office of Survivors at www4.va.gov/SURVIVORS/Office_ of_Survivors_Assistance.asp.or ask specific benefit questions at iris.va.gov/scripts/iris.cfg/

php.exe/enduser/home.php. Additional information for survivors is available at www.vba. va.gov/survivors/index.htm.

✔ **Apply for workers' compensation**

Workers' Compensation

All states have adopted workers' compensation laws. Although their details vary greatly, the general purpose of workers' compensation programs is to provide income to workers who are unable to work as a result of an injury or occupational disease while they are employed. While you are unable to work, you can receive a monetary benefit based on your average wage and number of dependents. In addition, your medical expenses related to the injury are paid by the employer or the employer's insurance company.

This section alerts you and your family to possible workers' compensation benefits available to your dependents. Ordinarily, if you die as the result of a work-incurred accident or occupational disease, your spouse and minor children are entitled to payments for a specified number of years or until the remarriage, whichever is sooner. Your dependent children are entitled to benefits until they reach a certain age.

Ordinarily, the laws also provide that your spouse or your estate are entitled to a specific funeral or death benefit.

It is important that your heirs are aware of any life-threatening injuries or occupational diseases that you incurred during the course of your employment. If your death is subsequently caused by such an injury or occupational disease, your dependents may be entitled to substantial monetary benefits.

In the checklists provided in this chapter, be sure to detail any of your medical problems that may be related to your employment.

✔ **Identify all available pension benefits**

Pensions

Many public and private employees are provided pensions through their jobs. Some pensions are entirely financed by the employer; others are co-financed by the employer and the employee. Pensions are a way to accumulate tax-advantaged savings that you can tap for a steady stream of income when you are no longer working. Pensions are considered to be *defined benefit plans* because you receive a specific amount of money when you retire that is defined in the terms of the pension. To calculate how much you will receive, your plan uses a formula that includes your salary history and how many years you were vested in the pension. At the time you begin to receive your pension you may have an opportunity to elect if your surviving spouse will continue to receive a portion of your pension after you die.

While many employers are no longer offering pensions, it's important for you to list all employment where you might have become eligible (vested) for a pension. You should check with all past employers that offered pension plans during your employment to determine if you or your survivors could receive any payments. Verify if survivor's benefits are available and check your designation of beneficiary.

✔ Manage disbursement from your retirement plans

Retirement Plans

In place of offering a pension, many employers offer *401(k) retirement plans* that defer taxes on both the contributions you and your employer make and the plan's earnings until you withdraw funds from the plan, usually when you retire. You will have to pay a 10 percent penalty on any money you withdraw before age 59 ½ in addition to income taxes.

These 401(k) plans are called *defined contribution* plans. You make a specific dollar contribution with each paycheck to a personal plan account. The plan invests your contributions (and your employer's, if any) in mutual funds or other investments that you select from the plan's menu of investment choices. Your plan account is credited with any returns on the investment. Unlike fixed pension payments, the amount you receive depends on the performance (which may be positive or negative) of your investments. At the time that you begin to withdraw money from your 401(k) you may have the option to take a reduced payment so your surviving spouse can continue to receive a portion of your retirement funds after your death if he or she outlives you.

Even if you are covered by a pension or 401(k) through your employment, you may also establish *individual retirement accounts* (IRAs). The law, as of 2011, allows a person who is under age 50 and who has earned income to deposit up to $5,000 into an IRA account each year ($6,000 for people over age 50). Contributions to your *Traditional* IRA may be wholly or partially tax deductible or nondeductible depending on whether you are also covered by a qualified pension plan or a 401(k), your tax filing status, and your income level. IRAs defer taxes on earnings from contributions until you withdraw funds, usually when you retire. Again, tax penalties apply to early withdrawals, except in certain circumstances. *Roth* IRA contributions, on the other hand, are not deductible, but withdrawals are tax-free.

Several other tax-deferred plans can also help you to defer taxes, until theoretically, you have reached an age where your earnings have begun to decline. For example, if you are self-employed you may establish a Keogh plan which allows for larger, tax-deferred yearly contributions and greater benefits than does an IRA. A SIMPLE IRA is a simplified plan, similar to a 401(k) plan, but with lower contribution limits and less costly administration. Another tax-deferred retirement for self-employed people is a simplified employee pension plan, or SEP, which is a type of IRA.

Required Minimum Distributions

Because your savings in retirement plans allow your money to grow without paying any taxes, the tax laws require you to start making withdrawals—and paying taxes—when you reach age 70 ½. If you haven't retired by age 70 ½ you must start taking withdrawals as soon as you retire. These withdrawals are called Required Minimum Distributions or RMDs. The RMD rules apply to all employer sponsored retirement plans, including profit-sharing plans, 401(k) plans, 403(b) plans, and 457(b) plans. The RMD rules also apply to traditional IRAs and IRA-based plans such as SEPs, SARSEPs, and SIMPLE IRAs. The tax penalties for failing to take the correct RMDs are a stiff 50 percent. The Roth IRA rules are different because you have paid taxes on the money you contributed to this type of IRA. The Internal Revenue Service (IRS) provides life expectancy tables and work sheets you can use to calculate the amount of your RMD in IRS Publication 590 at www.irs.gov/pub/irs-pdf/p590.pdf.

You, of course, can start taking withdrawals without penalty at any time after age 59 ½ and you can withdraw more than the required minimum amount.

✔ Verify the beneficiary designation on pension or retirement plans

Inheriting IRAs

If you die before age 70 ½ the beneficiaries of your 401(k) or IRA are also subject to special tax rules. Generally, the entire amount in your account must be distributed to an individual beneficiary either within 5 years of your death, or over the life of the beneficiary starting no later than one year following your death. Your beneficiaries will need to use the specific IRS life expectancy tables to calculate withdrawals and taxes and seek expert and timely advice on how best to manage this inheritance.

Regardless of what type of retirement plans you are participating in, it is critical that your heirs are aware of those plans. At your death, one of more of those plans may provide payments to your spouse and/or minor children, or may provide a substantial payment to a designated beneficiary or to your estate. On the other hand, a plan may provide nothing at all. Verify that you have made a designation of beneficiary for every plan.

In the checklists in this chapter, give your heirs information about any retirement assets in which you—and they—have an interest.

Heirs Checklist

✔ **Notify Social Security of the death**

You can report the death by calling 1-800-772-1213 or TTY 1-800-325-0778 from 7 a.m. to 7 p.m., Monday through Friday. Whenever you call, have the deceased person's Social Security number handy.

You have to return any Social Security checks that are received for the month in which the beneficiary died. For example, if the person dies in July, you must return the benefit paid in August. This means if the decedent receives a Social Security check after he or she dies, you have to return the un-cashed check. You will also need to notify the bank where the Social Security check is direct-deposited so the bank can return any Social Security payments as soon as possible.

✔ **Apply for Social Security survivor's benefits**

You will need:

- The deceased worker's Social Security card or a record of the number
- A copy of the death certificate
- The deceased worker's W-2 form (s) for the previous year or a copy of his or her last federal income tax return if self-employed. Without this information, those earnings may not yet be in the Social Security records and cannot be included when benefits are calculated.

✔ **Apply for Social Security survivor's benefits as a former spouse**

You will need:

- The deceased worker's Social Security card or a record of the number
- A copy of the divorce decree

✔ **Apply for Social Security benefits for any dependent children**

You will need:

- The deceased worker's Social Security card or a record of the number
- Your children's birth certificates and Social Security numbers

✔ **Apply for Medicare as an eligible spouse**

You will need:

- The deceased worker's Social Security card or a record of the number
- A copy of the marriage certificate

✔ **Apply for veterans burial benefits**

- You should have the funeral home contact the national cemetery where you want interment, or if you want a headstone, grave marker, or service medallion.
- If possible, the following information concerning the deceased should be provided when the cemetery is first contacted:
  - Full name and military rank
  - Branch of service
  - Social security number
  - Service number
  - VA claim number, if applicable
  - Date and place of birth
  - Date and place of death
  - Date of retirement or last separation from active duty
  - Copy of any military separation document, such as the Department of Defense Form 214 (DD-214). The discharge documents must specify active military duty and show that release from active duty was under other than dishonorable conditions.

✔ **Get a copy of the veteran's service record.** You can order this record, called the DD 214, at www.archives.gov/veterans/military-service-records/get-service-records. html.

✔ **Obtain a flag** by ordering at www4.va.gov/vaforms/ (VA Form 21-2008), or contact your local VA office or US Post Office. Most funeral directors will be able to help you obtain a flag.

✔ **Apply for burial benefits** by filling out VA Form 21-530, *Application for Burial Benefits*. You should attach a copy of the veteran's military discharge document (DD 214), death certificate, funeral and burial bills. They should show that you have paid them in full. You may download the form at www.va.gov/vaforms/.

✔ **Contact your local VA office** for assistance in obtaining burial benefits or go to www.cem.va.gov/.

✔ **Apply for veterans survivor's benefits**

- You will need the veteran's DD 214 number and a copy of the service record.
- Contact your local VA office for assistance in obtaining survivor benefits.

✔ **Apply for worker's compensation survivor's benefits**

- If the decedent was receiving worker's compensation at the time of death, inquire with the state compensation board to determine if a widow or dependent children can continue to receive benefits.

- If the decedent's death was caused by an injury or illness while working, inquire with the state compensation board to determine if a widow or dependent children are eligible for any compensation.

✔ **Apply for pension benefits for survivors**

- Contact each former employer who offered a pension to the decedent to claim any survivor's benefits.

✔ **Take disbursements from retirement plans**

- Contact the plan manager for any 401(k) to determine the steps surviving beneficiaries need to take.

CHAPTER 4
BENEFITS FOR SURVIVORS CHECKLISTS

Pensions

☐ I do not have any rights to a pension.

☐ I have the following pensions:

Pension source: _____

Name of payor: _____

Phone: _____ Fax: _____

Address: _____

_____

Email: _____ Website: _____

Pension ID #:_____

☐ There are benefits to survivors under this plan.

☐ There are no benefits to survivors under this plan.

Pension source: _____

Name of payor: _____

Phone: _____ Fax: _____

Address: _____

_____

Email: _____ Website: _____

Pension ID #:_____

☐ There are benefits to survivors under this plan.

☐ There are no benefits to survivors under this plan.

Retirement Plans

☐   I do not have an individual retirement account (IRA).

☐   I do have the following individual retirement accounts (IRA):

Name of IRA: _____

Name of institution: _____

Phone: _____ Fax: _____

Address: _____

_____

Email: _____ Website: _____

IRA account #: _____

☐   There are benefits to survivors under this plan.

☐   There are no benefits to survivors under this plan.

Name of IRA: _____

Name of institution: _____

Phone: _____ Fax: _____

Address: _____

_____

Email: _____ Website: _____

IRA account #: _____

☐   There are benefits to survivors under this plan.

☐   There are no benefits to survivors under this plan.

****

☐ I do not have a 401 (k) plan.

☐ I do have the following 401 (k) plans:

Name of 401 (k): _____

Name of institution: _____

Phone: _____ Fax: _____

Address: _____

_____

Email: _____ Website: _____

401 (k) account #: _____

☐ There are benefits to survivors under this plan.

☐ There are no benefits to survivors under this plan.

****

☐ I do not have a 403 (b) plan.

☐ I do have the following 403 (b) plans:

Name of 403 (b): _____

Name of institution: _____

Phone: _____ Fax: _____

Address: _____

_____

Email: _____ Website: _____

403 (b) account #: _____

☐ There are benefits to survivors under this plan.

☐ There are no benefits to survivors under this plan.

****

☐   I do not have a Keogh plan.

☐   I do have the following Keogh plan:

Name of Keogh: _____

Name of institution: _____

Phone: _____ Fax: _____

Address: _____

_____

Email: _____ Website: _____

Keogh account #: _____

☐   There are benefits to survivors under this plan.

☐   There are no benefits to survivors under this plan.

****

☐   I do not have a Simplified Employee Pension (SEP) plan.

☐   I do have the following SEP plan:

Name of SEP: _____

Name of institution: _____

Phone: _____ Fax: _____

Address: _____

_____

Email: _____ Website: _____

SEP account #: _____

☐   There are benefits to survivors under this plan.

☐   There are no benefits to survivors under this plan.

*****

☐   I do not have a Roth IRA.

☐   I do have the following Roth IRA:

Name of institution: _____

Phone: _____ Fax: _____

Address: _____

_____

Email: _____ Website: _____

Roth IRA account #: _____

☐   There are benefits to survivors under this plan.

☐   There are no benefits to survivors under this plan.

Social Security Benefits

☐　I have applied for Social Security benefits.

☐　I have not applied for Social Security benefits.

☐　I receive monthly Social Security benefits.

☐　I worked in the railroad industry at any time after January 1, 1937*

☐　I did not work in the railroad industry at any time after January 1, 1937

Name on Social Security card: _____

Social Security Number:_____

Type of monthly Social Security benefit: _____

(Disability, Retirement, Widow, etc.)

Monthly Social Security benefit amount: _____

This may affect the amount of Social Security you receive.

Veterans Benefits

☐ I did not serve in the military service of the United States.

☐ I served in the military service of the United States.

Full present name:_____

| | *First* | *Middle* | *Last* |

Name served under: _____

| | *First* | *Middle* | *Last* |

Entered Active Service			Separated		
Date	**Place**	**Service Number**	**Date**	**Place**	**Grade or Rank and Branch**

The following is a resume of my military career:

_____

_____

_____

_____

_____

_____

_____

_____

_____

Workers' Compensation

     ☐ I have never received workers' compensation benefits.

     ☐ I received the following workers' compensation benefits.

     ☐ My survivors may be eligible for workers' compensation benefits:

Employer: _____

Phone: _____ Fax: _____

Address: _____

_____

Email: _____ Website: _____

****

Date of injury or occupational disease:_____

Insurance company: _____

Phone: _____ Fax: _____

Address: _____

_____

Email: _____ Website: _____

Claim #:_____

Details of injury or occupational disease:

_____

_____

_____

****

In addition to the above, I received the following injuries or occupational diseases during my employment:

_____

_____

_____

Benefits: Other

The following miscellaneous information about public benefits may be of interest to my heirs:

_____

_____

_____

_____

_____

_____

_____

_____

_____

_____

_____

_____

_____

_____

_____

_____

_____

_____

_____

_____

_____

_____

_____

_____

_____

_____

_____

_____

_____

_____

_____

CHAPTER 5
BANKING AND SAVINGS

You have achieved success if you have lived well,
laughed often and loved much.

—Author Unknown

Banks used to be pretty plain vanilla. They offered checking and savings accounts, lent money to buy homes and cars, and maybe gave you a toaster when you opened a new account. Now you probably take advantage of a proliferation of services and have multiple types of accounts. In addition to a checking account and a savings account, you might have a certificate of deposit or money market account; carry a credit card or debit card with a PIN (personal identification number); use a financial advisor housed in the bank; rely on the automatic teller machine (ATM) to transfer funds between accounts and get cash; and pay your bills online. Thanks to interstate banking you may use different banks for different types of services. Your family needs to know about all the different types of accounts, where they are located, account numbers, PINs, etc.

My Checklist

Done	Need to Do	
☐	☐	Review how bank accounts are titled
☐	☐	List all banks where you do business
☐	☐	Assemble account numbers, and **with caution** your access PINs, ATM passwords, online banking usernames and passwords
☐	☐	Keep a record of all savings bonds
☐	☐	Make sure that your accounts are FDIC insured

☐   ☐   Keep original documents that are valuable or irreplaceable in a safe deposit box

☐   ☐   Be sure that someone knows where safe deposit boxes and keys are located

☐   ☐   List any credit unions where you do business

☐   ☐   Complete the checklists for Chapter 5

Banking and Savings Checklists

The checklists in Chapter 5 are set out in the following order:

- *Certificates of Deposit*
- *Checking Accounts*
- *Credit Unions*
- *Safe Deposit Boxes*
- *Savings Accounts*
- *Savings Bonds*
- *Banking and Savings: Other*

✔ **Review how bank accounts are titled**

Joint Ownership

How you title, or own, your various bank accounts can make a big difference for your heirs and who will be entitled them when you die. Among the possible ways you can own bank accounts are:

- *Individually:* Money retaining in this account will be distributed according to the terms of your will, or if you do not have a will, according to state law.

- *Agency or convenience account:* Money in this type of account can be accessed by the co-signer on the account but it does not belong to the co-signer on your death. This is the type of account most people should use if they want a family member to have access to the account to help pay bills when they are out of town or in the hospital. Money remaining in this account will be distributed according to the terms of your will, or if you do not have a will, according to state law.

- *Joint with right of survivorship:* As soon as you create this type of account all money in the account belongs to the co-owner and on your death automatically goes to the surviving co-owner. Adding a son, daughter or any other person to your account as joint owner is the same as making a gift of all money now on deposit and any future deposits. They can write checks for any purpose and could, in fact, withdraw it to zero and head for Alaska. For Medicaid purposes, adding a joint owner (other than your spouse) to an account is considered a transfer for less than fair market value and could result delaying your eligibility for Medicaid.

- *Pay on death (POD):* The person you name as beneficiary on this type of account automatically receives the balance in the account on your death, but has no right or authority to access the account until then. You can change the beneficiary, spend the money, or close the account at anytime.

✔ **List all banks where you do business**

Bank Accounts

Commercial banks offer a wide range of services. They handle savings and checking accounts and make short- and long-term loans for personal and business use. Many also provide estate and investment services.

Checking accounts are considered **demand deposits**. They allow you to draw checks payable to anyone. Many financial institutions now offer interest-bearing checking accounts, along with traditional fee-based checking plans. Banks may also offer over-draft protection by linking your checking account to your savings account. However, most banks charge stiff fees for each overdrawn check. Some may also charge a fee for over-draft protection. Be sure you understand what fees your bank will collect for over-draft protection or overdrawn checks.

Savings accounts are another type of **demand deposit**. In other words, as the depositor you have the right to demand, or to withdraw, any or all of your funds at any time during regular banking hours. Savings accounts pay you interest, which is noted, along with deposits and withdrawals, on a periodic statement or available on online. A *money market savings account* pays a higher rate of interest than a standard savings account but may require you to maintain a certain minimum balance in your account.

Certificates of deposit are **time deposits**. Customers who use certificates of deposit (CDs) agree to leave their money in the bank for a certain period—for example, two years. During that time, you may not withdraw those funds without incurring significant interest penalties. In return for having this long-term use of your money, banks generally pay a higher rate of interest.

Factors that affect the interest you can earn on your deposit accounts include your bank's method of compounding interest and of crediting the funds you put in the account and the money you withdraw. Banks can compound interest in a variety of ways so it pays to compare the details before buying a CD.

✔ **Assemble account numbers, and with caution your access PINs, ATM passwords, online banking usernames and passwords**

With today's multiple ways to do banking we can accumulate a sometimes bewildering collection of cards, personal identification numbers (PIN), passwords and usernames. These are the keys that you use to do your banking without ever entering a bank. You use them to get cash from an ATM or transfer funds and pay bills via online banking. However, they are also the very valuable keys that others can use to raid your accounts. You need to be extraordinarily careful about lending your ATM card, keeping your PIN private, and creating your passwords. For example, don't record your PIN on a piece of paper that you carry next to your debit card. Make sure that no one is looking over your shoulder when you enter your pass code at an ATM. Change your passwords frequently and make them something you can remember but is not obvious to a hacker, such as your mother's maiden name, birth date, or child's name. Identity thieves can easily find this information about you on the Internet, on social networking, school alumni, or genealogical sites.

✔ **Keep a record of all savings bonds**

Savings bonds are a very easy and secure way to save. You should make a list of each bond you are holding, the type series (E, EE, H, HH or I), denomination and issue date. Your heirs will find this list very helpful.

Depending on what type of savings bonds you have purchased and their maturity date, they may still be earning interest, or just sitting at maturity and no longer growing. There is more than $15 billion in unredeemed bonds. The Treasury Department does not send out notices when bonds have reached maturity and stopped earning interest, but it is easy to find out. You can use the Treasury Hunt tool on the web at www.savingsbonds.gov/indiv/tools/tools_treasuryhunt.htm to find out how much each bond is worth today.

✔ **Make sure that your accounts are FDIC insured**

Most banks insure their deposits through the Federal Deposit Insurance Corporation (FDIC). This governmental agency was established to protect people from losing their deposited assets if a bank fails. Up to $250,000 in your account is insured. On January 1, 2014, the standard insurance amount will return to $100,000 per depositor for all deposit accounts except certain retirement accounts (IRAs), which will remain at $250,000 per depositor. Be sure that your bank is insured by the FDIC and check the coverage limits on your accounts. Use the FDIC's EDIE (Electronic Deposit Insurance Estimator) calculator at www.fdic.gov/edie/index.html.

The FDIC insurance covers deposit accounts, including checking and savings accounts, money market deposit accounts, certificates of deposit and IRA accounts. It does not insure any other type of investment products you might purchase through your bank, such as mutual funds. If the total amount of your deposits exceeds the maximum amount of deposit insurance, to ensure that your funds are adequately covered, you can establish accounts in several name combinations (for example, husband alone, husband and wife, wife alone, husband and child, etc.) or, if necessary, in several banks.

✔ **Keep original documents that are valuable or irreplaceable in a safe deposit box**

✔ **Be sure that someone knows where the safe deposit boxes and keys are located**

Safe Deposit Boxes

Safe deposit boxes provide a place for storing valuables and documents at a small cost. Most banks rent safe deposit boxes or provide them as a free service along with a checking and/or savings account.

Safe deposit boxes come with a key. When you want to store items or access items, you must use both your key and a bank key simultaneously. Neither key alone will open the box for safety precautions. For further protection, you must also sign a slip each time you seek access to the box. Your signature will be compared to the signature that you placed on file when you first rented the box.

Safe deposit boxes protect your stocks, bonds, gold, silver, and other valuables from both physical burglary and fire damage. You may want to store in your safe deposit box important papers such as your marriage license, deeds to your real estate, car titles, and insurance policies. Be sure to record what is in your safe deposit box in the Records Checklist starting on page 24.

To protect you and the property in your box, banks restrict who can get into your box, as well as when and how they can do so. These security protections you want may hinder your family's need to have ready and easy access to your will or advance directives. So it is best not to put these documents in your safe deposit box.

A safe deposit box, like a bank account, may be owned in your name only or jointly. Joint ownership gives someone else access to your box should you need to get something out of the box when you are sick or out of town. In addition, joint ownership allows the co-owner access to the box after your death. Most states require the bank to seal a safe deposit box upon learning of the death of a co-owner. They then allow a surviving co-owner to open the box in the presence of a bank or state official, who will inventory the contents and deliver the inventory to the probate court. This process ensures that your assets are properly reported to the court and that the applicable inheritance taxes are applied to the contents of the box.

While joint owners of a safe deposit box have access to the box, access does not mean that they own the contents of the box. Putting your diamond ring into a safe deposit box does not change the ring's owner or make a gift of the ring to the joint owner. It will be part of your probate estate. If you have any questions about the rights of a co-owner to your box, check with your bank or your attorney.

✔ **List any credit unions where you do business**

Credit unions work very much like banks, although they are organized differently from banking institutions. Typically you need to be a member of some identified group to have an account, but in turn you become a part owner. Credit unions offer services that encourage you to save and often provide its members loans at lower rates. They offer checking and savings accounts (although they may be called share or draft accounts), credit cards, and online banking. Federally chartered credit unions are regulated by the National Credit Union Administration. Check to make sure your credit union account is insured by the National Credit Union Share Insurance Fund (NCUSIF). Like the FDIC, NCUSIF insures credit union accounts up to $250,000.

Heirs Checklist

✔ Be sure you know where the keys to any safe deposit boxes are located.

✔ Notify all banks or credit unions of the death and provide a copy of the death certificate.

✔ Some bank accounts may be temporarily frozen to make certain that no improper withdrawals are made before the estate is settled.

✔ Any Social Security check that is received in the month of the individual's death must be returned un-cashed to Social Security.

CHAPTER 5
BANKING AND SAVINGS CHECKLISTS

Certificates of Deposit

□ I do not have any certificates of deposit (CDs).

□ I have the following certificates of deposit (CDs):

Name of institution: _____

Phone: _____ Fax: _____

Address: _____

_____

Email: _____ Website: _____

Account #: _____

Maturity date: _____

Name of institution: _____

Phone: _____ Fax: _____

Address: _____

_____

Email: _____ Website: _____

Account #: _____

Maturity date: _____

Name of institution: _____

Phone: _____ Fax: _____

Address: _____

_____

Email: _____ Website: _____

Account #: _____

Maturity date: _____

Checking Accounts

☐   I do not have any checking accounts.

☐   I have the following checking accounts:

Name of institution: _____

Phone: _____ Fax: _____

Address: _____

_____

Email: _____ Website: _____

Account Number: _____

Debit card Number: _____

Name of institution: _____

Phone: _____ Fax: _____

Address: _____

_____

Email: _____ Website: _____

Account Number: _____

Debit card Number: _____

Name of institution: _____

Phone: _____ Fax: _____

Address: _____

_____

Email: _____ Website: _____

Account Number: _____

Debit card Number: _____

Name of institution: _____

Phone: _____ Fax: _____

Address: _____

_____

Email: _____ Website: _____

Account Number: _____

Debit card Number: _____

Credit Unions

☐ I do not have any credit union accounts.

☐ I have the following credit union accounts:

Name of institution: _____

Phone: _____ Fax: _____

Address: _____

_____

Email: _____ Website: _____

Account Number: _____

Name of institution: _____

Phone: _____ Fax: _____

Address: _____

_____

Email: _____ Website: _____

Account Number: _____

Safe Deposit Boxes

☐   I do not have any safe deposit boxes.

☐   I have the following safe deposit boxes:

Name of institution: _____

Phone: _____ Fax: _____

Address: _____

_____

Email: _____ Website: _____

Box number: _____

Key location: _____

Inventory:

_____

_____

_____

_____

_____

_____

_____

_____

Name of institution: _____

Phone: _____ Fax: _____

Address: _____

_____

Email: _____ Website: _____

Box number: _____

Key location: _____

Inventory:

_____

_____

_____

_____

_____

_____

_____

_____

Name of institution: _____

Phone: _____ Fax: _____

Address: _____

_____

Email: _____ Website: _____

Box number: _____

Key location: _____

Inventory:

_____

_____

_____

_____

_____

_____

_____

_____

Also record what you have in your safe deposit box on the Records Checklist beginning on page 24.

Savings Accounts

☐   I do not have any savings accounts.

☐   I have the following savings accounts:

Name of institution: _____

Phone: _____ Fax: _____

Address: _____

_____

Email: _____ Website: _____

Account Number: _____

Name of institution: _____

Phone: _____ Fax: _____

Address: _____

_____

Email: _____ Website: _____

Account Number: _____

Name of institution: _____

Phone: _____ Fax: _____

Address: _____

_____

Email: _____ Website: _____

Account Number: _____

Savings Bonds

☐   I do not have any savings bonds.

☐   I have the following savings bonds:

Series	Denomination	Serial Number	Issue Date

Banking and Savings: Other

The following miscellaneous information about my banking and savings may be of interest to my heirs:

_____

_____

_____

_____

_____

_____

_____

_____

_____

_____

_____

_____

_____

_____

_____

_____

_____

_____

_____

_____

_____

_____

_____

CHAPTER 6
INVESTMENTS

Life is either a daring adventure or nothing.

—Helen Keller

You have multiple ways you can invest for your own financial security, as well as to build up resources to leave for your family. Whether you actively follow the stock market, use online trading, rely on a financial adviser or have your nest egg in mutual funds and certificates of deposit, you most likely have two basic goals. One is to have enough money throughout your retirement to cover your expenses comfortably. The other is to be able to have enough left over to take care of your family and friends.

This chapter briefly covers some of the ways you can invest your money, including stocks, bonds and mutual funds. You can use the checklists in this chapter as a convenient place to record information about the securities you own, where you have investment accounts, and how your heirs can contact your brokers or financial advisers.

My Checklist

Done	Need to Do	
☐	☐	Periodically check to make sure that your investments match your investment objectives and are diversified
☐	☐	Check on the background of any financial professional
☐	☐	Organize statements you receive from your brokerage or investment adviser
☐	☐	Complete the checklists for Chapter 6

Investment Checklists

The checklists in Chapter 6 are set out in the following order:

- *Bonds*
- *Money Market Funds and Accounts*
- *Mutual Funds*
- *Stocks*
- *Investments: Other*

✔ **Periodically check to make sure your investments match your investment objectives and are deversified**

Stocks

When you own a stock, you own part of a company. Companies sell these pieces of ownership, known as shares, to raise money to finance their business. When you buy a stock you are basically betting that the company will grow. As the company does well, your stock generally increases in value. You can earn money on your investment either when the price of the stock rises or if the company shares company profits by paying a dividend. If the company does poorly, you can lose some or all of the money you paid for the share.

There are over 3,000 companies listed on the New York Stock Exchange that you can invest in. Stocks are categorized in multiple ways: by industry (auto, biotechnology); by market sector (utilities, health care); or geography (U.S., Asian). They can also be categorized by size, as in large-capitalization, or large-cap (generally companies worth more than $5 billion), mid-cap ($1 to $5 billion), or small-cap ($250 million to $1 billion). Another way to group stocks is based on financial experts' perception of the company's basic financial health and historical performance. These categories include growth stocks, value stocks, or income stocks. Knowing how a particular company's stocks are categorized helps you diversify your investments in different types of companies. Diversification reduces your risk of losing money.

Bonds

When you buy a bond, you loan money to a company or government entity. The entity commits to paying you interest at a fix rate for the life of the loan and to return to you the value of the loan by a certain date, called the maturity date. When you invest in a bond you are taking the risk that the borrower may not be able to pay the interest or the principal. You also run the risk that if interest rates rise and you need to sell the bond, your bond may lose value. This is because other investors can buy higher rate bonds, so you have to sell yours at a lower price to attract a buyer. If you buy a *callable* bond, the company has the right to pay you back before the maturity date. This is normally done when the company can borrow at a cheaper rate.

Bonds issued by the federal government are the safest. Treasury bills, notes and bonds are available with maturities ranging from one to thirty years. They can be easily sold, but like all bonds their values rise and fall as interest rates change. You pay no federal income tax on the interest you earn.

State and local governments also issue bonds to pay for things like roads, schools, and public safety. You pay no federal income tax on the interest, and may not have to pay state taxes if you live in the area where the bond is issued. Because of this tax advantage, the interest rates are lower than on other types of bonds.

Mutual Funds

When you buy shares of a mutual fund, you own a bit of various stocks, bonds, or other types of investments in the fund. Buying shares of a mutual fund helps you diversify because you are spreading the risk of losing your money among many different investments. Investments within a mutual fund are chosen by a professional manager based on the fund's investment objectives. The fund's objectives, set out in a public document called a prospectus, might be to own growth stock, government bonds, or invest in a particular industry, such as pharmaceuticals.

Morningstar, a provider of mutual fund research, tracks over 15,000 mutual funds so you have many to choose from. Some of the common types of mutual funds are:

- Stock funds that invest in the stocks of many companies;
- Bond funds that are a collection of bonds purchased with pooled money from many investors;
- Money market funds that include short-term, low-risk loans;
- Index funds that are made up of all the securities in a particular index, such as the Standard & Poor's 500 index;
- Balanced funds that include a mix of stocks and bonds;
- Life cycle funds, or target retirement date funds, that are designed to increase the percentage of bonds in relation to stocks as the investor gets closer to retirement age.

Money market accounts and money market funds have significant differences. A *money market account* is a type of saving account you have at a financial institution. Typically the financial institution will pay a higher rate of interest than on regular savings accounts. You are able to make withdrawals at any time and can access the funds through ATM withdrawals or by writing a check. As with other accounts in FDIC-insured banks your money would be insured up to $250,000. You may have to maintain a minimum amount to avoid fees and be restricted on how many withdraws you can make in a month. A **money market fund** is a type of mutual fund that is required by law to invest in low-risk, short-term debt. These funds are not insured.

As with any type of investment you need to carefully match the fund's objectives with your own investment objectives. You also need to pay attention to the fund's fees. High fees or expense ratios can reduce your earnings.

Financial Advisers

Many different types of professionals can assist you in managing your investments, developing an investment strategy, or in setting up a withdrawal plan. Which type of professional you should consult depends on what investment help you need.

Financial planners generally take a broad view of your financial affairs. They may develop a comprehensive plan to meet your investment goals or generally advise you on financial matters. They may also manage your investment portfolio.

Fee only advisers are paid a specific fee for each service.

Investment advisers generally focus on managing your investments. Most are paid by taking a percentage of the assets they manage for you.

Stockbrokers buy and sell stocks and bonds and are paid by commissions on the trades they make for you. Some brokers also provide financial planning services.

Insurance agents can help you with your insurance needs including health, long-term care and life insurance as well as annuities.

Certified Public Accountant (CPA) is licensed by a state to offer a variety of accounting services including tax preparation, financial audits, business valuations and succession planning for small businesses.

Estate planning attorneys can draft legal documents for you including your will and power of attorney, or develop wealth transfer strategies to ensure your estate passes to your heirs in the most tax-efficient manner.

✔ **Check on the background of any financial professional**

Before hiring any financial professional, always inquire as to what licenses or certifications they hold, the types of services they offer, the typical clients they work with, and how they will be compensated. You should always know in advance how you are going to pay for your financial professional's services. Get in writing whether you are paying a retainer fee upfront, being charged a set fee for each service, or having a percentage deducted from any transaction.

Use www.finra.org/brokercheck for information about brokerages, brokers, and investment advisers. The Securities and Exchange Commission provides investment adviser information at www.adviserinfo.sec.gov. Go to www.naic.org to check on insurance agents. You will find disciplinary actions taken against CPAs by the American Institute of CPAs at www.aicpa.org/FORTHEPUBLIC/DISCIPLINARYACTIONS/Pages/default.aspx. Check on Certified Financial Planners at www.cfp.net/search. Information about attorneys can be found at your state bar association's website.

✔ **Organize statements you receive from your brokerage or investment adviser**

While much investing can be done online, keeping track of your investments still involves lots of paper. You can accumulate a small mountain of paper associated with prospectuses, proxy notices, annual reports, and monthly and quarterly statements. A big three-ring binder can be an efficient way to assemble statements and other notices. By organizing your investment information you will lessen the work that your family will have to do when they need to manage your investments.

Heirs Checklist

✔ Promptly contact any investment professionals so that accounts can be valued as of the date of death for tax purposes.

✔ Notify any financial advisers or stock brokers to change ownership of joint investment accounts.

✔ Suspend any open brokerage orders.

CHAPTER 6
INVESTMENTS CHECKLISTS

Bonds

☐ I do not have any bonds or bond funds.

☐ I have the following bonds or bond funds:

Name of institution/brokerage firm: _____

Phone: _____ Fax: _____

Address: _____

_____

Email: _____ Website: _____

Account Number: _____

Name of institution/brokerage firm: _____

Phone: _____ Fax: _____

Address: _____

_____

Email: _____ Website: _____

Account Number: _____

Name of institution/brokerage firm: _____

Phone: _____ Fax: _____

Address: _____

_____

Email: _____ Website: _____

Account Number: _____

Money Market Funds and Accounts

☐   I do not have any money market funds.

☐   I have the following money market funds:

Name of institution/brokerage firm: _____

Phone: _____ Fax: _____

Address: _____

_____

Email: _____ Website: _____

Account Number: _____

Name of institution/brokerage firm: _____

Phone: _____ Fax: _____

Address: _____

_____

Email: _____ Website: _____

Account Number: _____

☐   I do not have any money market accounts.

☐   I have the following money market accounts:

Name of institution/brokerage firm: _____

Phone: _____ Fax: _____

Address: _____

_____

Email: _____ Website: _____

Account Number: _____

Mutual Funds

□ I do not have any mutual funds.

□ I have the following mutual funds:

Name of institution/brokerage firm: _____

Phone: _____ Fax: _____

Address: _____

_____

Email: _____ Website: _____

Account Number: _____

Name of institution/brokerage firm: _____

Phone: _____ Fax: _____

Address: _____

_____

Email: _____ Website: _____

Account Number: _____

Name of institution/brokerage firm: _____

Phone: _____ Fax: _____

Address: _____

_____

Email: _____ Website: _____

Account Number: _____

Stocks

☐   I do not have any stocks.

☐   I have the following stocks:

Name of institution/brokerage firm: _____

Phone: _____ Fax: _____

Address: _____

_____

Email: _____ Website: _____

Account Number: _____

Name of institution/brokerage firm: _____

Phone: _____ Fax: _____

Address: _____

_____

Email: _____ Website: _____

Account Number: _____

Name of institution/brokerage firm: _____

Phone: _____ Fax: _____

Address: _____

_____

Email: _____ Website: _____

Account Number: _____

Investments: Other

The following miscellaneous information about my investments may be of interest to my heirs:

_____

_____

_____

_____

_____

_____

_____

_____

_____

_____

_____

_____

_____

_____

_____

_____

_____

_____

_____

_____

_____

_____

_____

_____

_____

_____

_____

_____

CHAPTER 7
REAL ESTATE

*He is a wise man who does not grieve for the things
which he has not, but rejoices for those which he has.*

—Marcel Proust

Real estate, or **real property,** is everything permanently attached to the land that you own. When you buy real estate you not only purchase soil, but also the trees, shrubs, fences, and buildings that are on it. Your home is most likely the most important real estate you own.

My Checklist

Done	Need to Do	
☐	☐	Assemble copies of the deeds to all real estate
☐	☐	Review how your property is titled
☐	☐	Discuss your real estate ownership and taxes with a tax adviser or estate planner
☐	☐	Determine if your property qualifies for tax relief
☐	☐	Consolidate all commercial property records
☐	☐	Obtain a copy of your Master Deed and condominium association documents
☐	☐	Consolidate all farm land records
☐	☐	Obtain a copy of your timeshare contract
☐	☐	Complete the checklists for Chapter 7

Real Estate Checklists

The checklists in Chapter 7 are set out in the following order:

- *Commercial*
- *Condominium*
- *Farm Land*
- *Residence*
- *Timeshare*
- *Real Estate: Other*

✔ Assemble copies of the deeds to all real estate

You can tell how you own property by looking at the deed to that piece of real estate. If you do not have a copy of the deed, you can get a copy from the clerk of the land records in the county where the property is located. You will want to keep copies of each deed in your safe deposit box.

✔ Review how your property is titled

There are many different ways that you can own, or hold title, to real estate. How you hold title has a significant impact on your heirs and how your property will be distributed at your death. Take, for example, all the ways you can own your home. You can own it in your own name or jointly with others. You can keep the right to live in your home for as long as you live, even after giving ownership to someone else. You can own the space where you live but not the building. Or a trust could own your home.

Individual Ownership

You can own real property *individually* in your own name. This means that you alone have the right to sell it, rent it, transfer it by will, and use it in any legal way. You need to state in your will who you want to inherit this property. If you do not have a will, your state's law of *intestacy* will determine who gets it. Intestacy law sets up a priority scheme of inheritance. To a degree it tries to anticipate who the typical person would want to inherit their property if they had gotten around to writing a will. You should check to see what your state's priority scheme is, but typically real estate would first go to a spouse, and if no spouse then to children, and if no children then to parents, then to siblings, and so forth out multiple branches of the family tree to the closest next of kin. Most intestacy laws also include rules of what to do when there are bumps in the family tree such as adopted children, deceased children with living children, or multiple marriages. Only if no next of kin can be located does the state get your property, called *escheat* to the state.

Joint Ownership

There are two ways you can own real estate with someone else. Your deed establishes whether they are joint owners or common owners. ***Joint owners with right of survivorship*** have equal ownership and rights to use and enjoy the property. When one of the joint owners dies, the surviving owner or owners automatically continue to own the property. The last surviving owner ends up as the sole owner of the property. This last owner can then leave that property by will, or it will be distributed through intestacy rules. All joint owners must agree to sell or mortgage the property.

✔ **Discuss your real estate ownership and taxes with a tax adviser or estate planner**

Adding a Child to a Deed

Joint ownership with right of survivorship is typically the way that spouses own their home because it is a convenient way to avoid the need to probate that property when the first spouse dies. On the other hand, adding a child to a deed because you want the child to inherit your home is fraught with possible negative consequences, both to you and your child. You cannot sell your home, take out a home equity loan or get a mortgage without your child's consent. You will not be able to get a reverse mortgage (unless your child is over age 62). If your child is sued, gets a divorce, or goes into bankruptcy, your jointly owned home will be involved in those legal entanglements.

By adding a child to your deed as a joint owner you are making a gift of the value of the home, which has tax and Medicaid complications. You may need to declare the gift to the IRS, by preparing gift-tax returns. Refer to IRS Publication 950 at www.irs.gov/publications/p950/ar02.html for more details or consult with your attorney. While it may at first sound attractive to your child that he or she is getting the house now rather than having to wait to inherit it after you die, the different tax consequences between getting it now and waiting until later may make the idea less inviting—to both of you.

When you make a gift of your home by adding your child as a joint owner, your child gets the same basis as you had at the time you make the gift. ***Basis*** is important in determining the amount of taxes that will be due when the house is sold. As an example, you originally purchased your home for $250,000. It has increased in value to $400,000 at the time you make the gift. You have made a gift worth $150,000. If the house is worth $500,000 when you die, your heirs get what is called stepped up basis, or the value of the house on the date of death. If your daughter ***inherited*** the home, she would have a basis of $500,000, and a gain of only $100,000, if she later sells it for $600,000. If your son was ***gifted*** the house, he would have a basis of $125,000 for the half he was gifted (half of the original basis of $250,000) and $250,000 on the half he inherited (half of the $500,000 value at date of death) for a total basis of $375,000. If he sells at $600,000 he would have a gain of $225,000. At a 15% capital gains rate the difference in tax liability is $15,000 versus $33,750.

Note: At the time this was written Congress was revisiting the step-up basis rules.

Gifting ownership of your home may also prevent or delay you from being eligible for Medicaid if you need to go into a nursing home. Medicaid rules consider that a gift made within five years of an application for Medicaid is a transfer for less than fair market value. It will assess an eligibility penalty that is calculated by dividing the value of the transfer by the state's average nursing facility private pay rate to determine how many months you have to wait before you are eligible for Medicaid. You can make gifts to your spouse without this penalty. Additionally, Medicaid does not include up to $500,000 of the value of your home in determining the maximum amount of resources you can have to be Medicaid eligible.

Note: Medicaid eligibility rules frequently change and vary from state to state. Check with an attorney experienced with your state's Medicaid rules before making any gift.

Common Ownership

Ownership in common (called tenants in common) is the other primary way to own real estate with someone else. The key difference is what happens to the share of ownership when a common owner dies. Unlike joint ownership with right of survivorship, the surviving owner does not inherit any greater interest or share in the property. The common owner's share passes to the decedent's estate. Siblings who own property together, such as a beach house, may want to consider ownership in common so that each sibling's interest will pass down to their own children, rather than to the sibling or nieces and nephews.

Community Property

For spouses in nine states (Arizona, California, Idaho, Louisiana, Nevada, New Mexico, Texas, Washington, and Wisconsin) all property acquired during the marriage automatically becomes community property. The laws vary in each of these states, but the basic theory is that each spouse acquires an equal interest in the property. When a husband or wife dies only one-half of the marital property is inheritable since the surviving spouse owns in his or her own right one-half of the marital property. Each spouse has the right to assign by will the ownership of their portion of the community property. Property that either spouse brought into the marriage or inherits is considered separate property.

✔ Determine if your property qualifies for tax relief

Depending on where you live you may be eligible for property tax relief on your residence. Most states or counties offer some reduction in taxes based on the age, income, disability, or military status of the homeowner. You can contact your local agency where you pay taxes, your state department of revenue or taxation, or your local area agency on aging to find out if you are eligible. Check out the Lincoln Institute of Land Policy to find out what special tax policies are available in your state. Go to www.lincolninst.edu, click on "Resources & Tools," then "Significant Features of the Property Tax."

✔ Consolidate all commercial property records

In addition to the deeds to any commercial property that you own, you should organize all the other documents that someone would need to locate should they have to take over management of the property tomorrow. At a minimum, you should have your business plan, all contracts, lease agreements, account records, bank statements, and tax records consolidated for each property.

✔ Obtain a copy of your Master Deed and condominium association documents

A condominium is a special form of ownership. Typically a condominium owner individually owns a specific unit as well as jointly owns with all the other unit owners the common areas such as the public hallways, lobby, and recreational areas. You should have copy of the Master Deed or Declaration, which describes the space that you own, the common areas, and any restrictions on how you can use or modify your unit or the common areas. A copy of the Master Deed that you signed should be on file in your local court house.

You should also have a copy of your condominium association documents. The condominium association includes all the unit owners who manage the condominium through an elected board of directors. Your condominium association may also have a separate set of Bylaws and/or Rules that further set out how the condominium is to be managed, pet restrictions, color choices, as well as how monthly unit fees are assessed.

✔ Consolidate all farm land records

As with any income producing property, you should maintain in logical order any records relating to the management of your farm property. These records could include all business plans, land leases, easements, assessments, crop insurance policies, tax records, herd records for any livestock, equipment leases or invoices, and inventory of all equipment.

✔ Obtain a copy of your timeshare contract

A timeshare is a way to own the right to use property, rather than direct ownership of the property. With most timeshares, multiple people have the right to use the same property, with each having a specific period of time when they have exclusive use of the property. You may purchase a specific week in a specific unit, or be able to negotiate a rotating time schedule or trade your share for use of multiple properties. Because there are so many variations on the timeshare concept, your contract is very important. It will explain to you and your family what happens to the timeshare on your death.

Heirs Checklist

✔ Secure all property for safety and be sure it is insured.

✔ Change any locks as necessary.

✔ Consider notifying law enforcement to keep an eye on the property if the property will remain vacant for any period of time.

✔ Consult with an attorney about the need to change the title to any property if you are a surviving joint owner.

✔ Consult with an attorney about the rights you have as a survivor with respect to condominium property or timeshares.

CHAPTER 7
REAL ESTATE CHECKLISTS

Commercial

- ☐ I do not own any commercial property.
- ☐ I own the following commercial property:

Property address:_____

_____

Township: _____ County: _____

My ownership interest is:

- ☐ Sole
- ☐ Community property
- ☐ Joint with right of survivorship
- ☐ Tenant in common

With:

_____

_____

Purchase price: _____

- ☐ I do not owe any money on the property.
- ☐ I owe money on the property as follows:

Financial Institution/Loan Servicer: _____

Phone: _____ Fax: _____

Address: _____

_____

Email: _____ Website: _____

Condominium

☐   I do not own any condominium property.

☐   I own the following condominium property:

Property address:_____

_____

Township: _____ County: _____

My condominium association can be contacted:

Name: _____

Phone: _____ Fax: _____

Address: _____

_____

Email: _____

My condominium association dues are:

_____

Purchase price: _____

☐   I do not owe any money on the condominium.

☐   I owe money on the condominium as follows:

Financial Institution/Mortgage Servicer: _____

Phone: _____ Fax: _____

Address: _____

_____

Email: _____ Website: _____

Type of Mortgage:_____

Balance due: _____ Monthly payment: _____

Farm Land

    ☐   I do not own any farm land.

    ☐   I own the following farm land:

Property address:_____

_____

Township: _____ County: _____

My ownership interest is:

    ☐   Sole

    ☐   Community property

    ☐   Joint with right of survivorship

    ☐   Tenant in common

With:

_____

_____

Purchase price: _____

    ☐   I do not owe any money on the real estate.

    ☐   I owe money on the real estate as follows:

Financial Institution/Mortgage Servicer: _____

Phone: _____ Fax: _____

Address: _____

_____

Email: _____ Website: _____

Type of loan: _____

Balance due: _____ Monthly payment: _____

Residence

    ☐ I do not own any residential property.

    ☐ I own the following residential property:

Property address:_____

_____

Township: _____ County: _____

My ownership interest is:

    ☐ Sole

    ☐ Community property

    ☐ Joint with right of survivorship

    ☐ Tenant in common

With:

_____

_____

Purchase price: _____

    ☐ I do not owe any money on my residence.

    ☐ I owe money on my residence as follows:

Financial Institution/Mortgage Servicer: _____

Phone: _____ Fax: _____

Address: _____

_____

Email: _____ Website: _____

Type of mortgage:_____

Balance due: _____ Monthly payment: _____

Timeshare

☐   I do not own any timeshare property.

☐   I own the following timeshare property:

Property address:_____

_____

Type Share: _____ County: _____

Purchase price: _____

☐   I do not owe any money on the timeshare.

☐   I owe money on the timeshare as follows:

Financial Institution/Mortgage Servicer: _____

Phone: _____ Fax: _____

Address: _____

_____

Email: _____ Website: _____

Balance due: _____ Monthly payment: _____

My annual maintenance fee is $ _____. It is due on _____

It is due to:

Name: _____

Phone: _____ Fax: _____

Address: _____

_____

Email: _____

Real Estate: Other

The following miscellaneous information about my real estate may be of interest to my heirs:

_____

_____

_____

_____

_____

_____

_____

_____

_____

_____

_____

_____

_____

_____

_____

_____

_____

_____

_____

_____

_____

_____

_____

_____

_____

_____

_____

_____

CHAPTER 8
OTHER ASSETS AND DEBTS

*Always do right- this will gratify some and
astonish the rest.*

—Mark Twain

The preceding chapters provided checklists for you to record your checking and savings accounts, insurance, investments, and real estate. This chapter is included to provide you with pages to list your various other assets and debts.

My Checklist

To Do	Done	
☐	☐	Assemble receipts or appraisals for higher-valued possessions
☐	☐	Photograph or videotape special possessions
☐	☐	Write down stories about how you acquired special possessions
☐	☐	Put the terms of any personals loans in writing
☐	☐	List contact information for credit cards
☐	☐	Consider whether a reverse mortgage would be appropriate
☐	☐	Complete the checklists for Chapter 8

Other Assets and Debts Checklists

The checklists in Chapter 8 are set out in the following order:

- *Business Interests*
- *Copyrights, Patents, Royalties, and Trusts*
- *Credit Cards*

- *Debts*
- *Lawsuits and Judgments*
- *Personal Property*
- *Reverse Mortgage*
- *Assets and Debts: Other*

Assets

Because checklists cannot be tailor-made to cover all the things everyone might have, this chapter provides places to list a number of common assets—motor vehicles, frequent flyer miles, as well as names and addresses of people to whom you owe money, if you have a reverse mortgage, business interests, whether you are the beneficiary of a trust, whether you have an interest in a trust or real estate at the death of another person, and information regarding any claims or lawsuits you may have against other persons—or they against you.

Use these checklists to record information about any of these possible assets. You may be surprised at what you have. Information about these not so obvious assets will be invaluable to your family. Executors don't like surprises when it comes time to finalize an estate. This information can help avoid surprises. It may save time and money in completing an inventory.

✔ Assemble receipts or appraisals for higher-valued possessions

Additional space is provided for you to list any assets of value you may own. Make sure that you list any items of furniture that have great value. The same applies to expensive paintings and artwork, coin or stamp collections, valuable jewelry, etc. You don't need to list everything, but do include items of special interest or value. Receipts or appraisals are important in establishing the value of your special possessions.

✔ Photograph or videotape special possessions

Now is a good time to inventory your special possessions. One way to do this is to take photographs or even make a video as you walk through your rooms and cabinets. After you have documented what you have, put the photo negatives, a disk with the digital pictures, or the video tape in your safe deposit box or other fire proof storage. This will be invaluable not only to your executor, but also if you should have a home fire, storm damage, or house burglary. Having these pictures will make it so much easier to file an insurance claim for loss or theft.

✔ Write down stories about how you acquired special possessions

After you have taken the photos, go the extra step to explain any interesting stories about how you acquired special items. Only you will be able to pass on the history of the silver bowl you got as a wedding present from Aunt Tully, or the story of how you haggled with a street merchant for the painting in the dining room. Be sure your family knows that the opal ring came from your maternal grandmother, while the pocket watch was Great Uncle Randolph's. Years from now your grandkids won't be able to remember if the family portrait in the bedroom is from your grandmother's side of the family or your spouse's. A post-it note you put on the back that says when the picture was taken and who's in the picture will be greatly appreciated. If you are not sure, check with others who might help you to get the facts captured now. The next generation will have an even harder time tracking the information down. The same advice applies to that box where you have stored family photographs. You'll have fun and raise some fond memories as you go through to label who's in the pictures and where they were taken.

Debts

✔ Put the terms of any personal loans in writing

Your heirs may have little knowledge of your debts. While you do not need to list fluctuating monthly bills, if you have borrowed money from a relative, friend, or associate, tell your heirs about it. Also, if you have lent money to a friend or family member, be sure to record that information. All personal loans should be in writing so both you and your borrower know the terms for paying back the money. If you intend to forgive any debts at your death, be sure to put your intentions in writing. Forgiving a loan becomes a gift, which can have consequences in settling your estate, determining taxes, and being eligible for Medicaid.

✔ List contact information for credit cards

It's important that you have a list of all your credit card accounts. You need to have this list readily available now in case you need to report that a card has been lost or stolen. Your family needs to know this information so they will know what companies to contact after your death. Sad as it may sound, identity thieves are known to read obituaries to seek potential victims.

✔ Consider whether a reverse mortgage would be appropriate

Reverse Mortgage

A reverse mortgage is a loan against your home that requires no repayment for as long as you live there. It is offered by the FHA (Federal Housing Administration) to homeowners ages 62 or older. These federally-insured and regulated loans are called Home Equity Conversion Mortgages or HECMs. It is different from other types of loans because the borrower does not make payments during the loan.

A reverse mortgage is one option for you to consider if you want to use the equity in your home to help meet your daily living or medical expenses. You can select whether you want to receive the loan proceeds as a lump sum or as monthly disbursements. Depending on your circumstances and needs, a reverse mortgage may allow you to stay financially secure in your home because you don't have to worry about a mortgage payment.

If you are eligible you can get a reverse mortgage, like a traditional mortgage, from a private lender (such as a bank) that is secured by the equity in your house. However, unlike a traditional mortgage that gets smaller as loan payments are made, the reverse mortgage typically gets larger over time. The reason the mortgage gets larger is that compound interest on the amount borrowed continues to increase the longer the loan is in place. You do not need to make payments until you die, move, or sell your home. Then the entire loan must be paid back. This usually means that the home must be sold instead of being passed on to your family.

Why is this? If your increasing loan balance grows so it equals or exceeds the value of your home, then your total debt is limited to your home's value, if your home is sold to repay the loan. However, if your family wishes to keep the home after you die or you move and pay off the loan with other proceeds, such as a new mortgage, you or your estate must pay the full loan balance. Your heirs do not have any personal liability for repaying the loan if your home is not sold, but the loan has to be paid.

Reverse mortgages are only available if the youngest homeowner is over the age of 62. It is easier to qualify for a reverse mortgage than a traditional mortgage because the bank does not need to consider your income or credit rating before qualifying you for the loan. However, because reverse mortgages are quite different from any other loan, you need to do your homework carefully and thoroughly before considering one. As a protection to you so you understand all the consequences and benefits of a reverse mortgage, you must receive independent counseling by a certified counselor before the lender can issue the loan. You can find a list of certified HECM counselors at www.hud.gov/offices/hsg/sfh/hecm/hecmlist.cfm.

While the benefits of using your home's equity to met expenses can be substantial, the upfront and ongoing costs involved in a reverse mortgage are high. These fees, including an origination fee, mortgage insurance premium, closing costs, and loan servicing fees, can amount to thousands of dollars. Unless you are facing a financial emergency, you may want to consider other options before taking out a reverse mortgage. Your family needs to know if you have a reverse mortgage on your home and realize that the loan must be repaid as soon as you die, move, or sell your home.

Heirs Checklist

✔ Notify the company servicing any reverse mortgage as soon as possible to make arrangement to pay off the loan. Interest continues to accrue until the loan is paid off so it is important to act quickly.

✔ Read *Borrowing Against Your Home* at http://www.aarp.org/revmort under "Resources" for more information about what you need to do to pay off a reverse mortgage.

✔ Notify all credit card companies and each credit reporting company (Experian, TransUnion and Equifax) so they can flag the accounts that the owner is deceased. This can help limit the opportunity for identity theft of the deceased person's credit information.

✔ Offer to help photograph or videotape special personal possessions.

CHAPTER 8
OTHER ASSETS AND DEBTS CHECKLISTS

Business Interests

☐　I do not have any business interests.

☐　I have the following business interests:

Business name: _____

Type of business:_____

Corporation: _____

Partners: _____

% of ownership: _____

Phone: _____ Fax: _____

Address: _____

_____

Email: _____ Website: _____

Business name: _____

Type of business:_____

Corporation: _____

Partners: _____

% of ownership: _____

Phone: _____ Fax: _____

Address: _____

_____

Email: _____ Website: _____

Copyrights, Patents, Royalties, and Trusts

☐   I do not have any patents or copyrights.

☐   I have the following patents or copyrights:

Description	Date Granted	Status	Patent or Copyright Number	Termination Date

****

☐   I do not have any royalty agreements.

☐   I have the following royalty agreements:

Description	Date Granted	Status	Royalty Amount	Payment Dates

☐ I am not the beneficiary of any trust agreements.

☐ I am the beneficiary of the following trust agreements:

Description	Date Granted	Trustee	Beneficiary Type

Credit Cards

☐   I do not have any credit cards.

☐   I have the following credit cards:

Credit Card Company	Contact Information	Card Number

Debts

☐ The following persons owe me money:

Name of Debtor	Contact Information	Amount Due

☐ I do not owe anyone any money.

☐ I owe the following persons money:

To Whom	For What	Contact Information	Amount Due

Lawsuits and Judgments

☐   I do not have any lawsuits or legal claims pending.

☐   I have the following lawsuits or legal claims pending:

Description	Date Granted	Accountant	Attorney	Type Lawsuit or Legal Claim

****

☐   I do not have any uncollected legal judgments pending.

☐   I have the following uncollected legal judgments pending:

Description	Date Granted	Accountant	Attorney	Type Legal Judgment

Personal Property

☐ I do not own any collectibles.

☐ I own the following collectibles:

Collectible	Description	Value

☐ I do not have any frequent flier mileage.

☐ I have frequent flier mileage with the following airlines and companies:

Airline/Company	Frequent Flyer Number	Contact Information

☐ I do not have any miscellaneous assets.

☐ I have the following miscellaneous assets, special possessions, antiques, jewelery, art, silver, etc.

Description	Location	Estimated Value	Significance

☐ I do not have any items in public storage.

☐ I have the following items in public storage:

Public Storage	Contents	Location

☐ I do not own any vehicles.

☐ I own the following vehicles:

Vehicle Type	Description	Balance Due

☐ I do not have any debts.

☐ I have the following debts:

Debt	Contact Information	Payment Due Dates	Amount Due

Reverse Mortgage

☐   I do not have a reverse mortgage

☐   I do have the following reverse mortgage:

Property Address: _____

_____

Township: _____ County: _____

Financial Institution: _____

Phone: _____ Fax: _____

Address: _____

_____

Email: _____ Website: _____

Type of reverse mortgage:_____

Mortgage Account #:_____

Assets and Debts: Other

The following miscellaneous information about my assets or debts may be of interest to my heirs:

_____

_____

_____

_____

_____

_____

_____

_____

_____

_____

_____

_____

_____

_____

_____

_____

_____

_____

_____

_____

_____

_____

_____

_____

_____

_____

_____

_____

CHAPTER 9
WILLS, TRUST AGREEMENTS, AND POWERS OF ATTORNEY

It matters not how strait the gate,
How charged with punishments the scroll.
I am the master of my fate:
I am the captain of my soul.

—William Ernest Henley

The word *estate* brings to mind mansions, fancy cars, and lots of money. But don't be fooled. Anyone with a home, car, bank account, investments, or even a set of china or silver has an estate. You'll want to do some estate planning so your wishes for how your estate is distributed after your death will be in place.

My Checklist

Done	Need to Do	
☐	☐	Consult with an estate planning expert
☐	☐	Inventory all of your assets
☐	☐	Consult with a tax advisor
☐	☐	Document any major financial gifts
☐	☐	Discuss your estate plan with your executor
☐	☐	Identify a source of funding for any anticipated estate settlement fees
☐	☐	Prepare or review your will

☐ ☐ Prepare any necessary codicils to your will

☐ ☐ Consider if a living trust should be part of your estate plan

☐ ☐ Select an agent to manage your financial affairs

☐ ☐ Prepare a letter of instruction

Wills, Trust Agreements, and Powers of Attorney Checklists

The checklists in Chapter 9 are set out in the following order:

- *Codicils*
- *Durable Power of Attorney*
- *Gifts*
- *Letter of Instruction*
- *Living Trust*
- *Will*
- *Wills, Trust Agreements, and Powers of Attorneys: Other*

✔ **Consult with an estate planning expert**

Types of Estates

What you own at the time of your death can be grouped into different categories depending on various factors. In the very biggest category there's your "estate" which is everything that you own at the time of your death. There's your *probate estate* which includes those things that will be distributed according to your will or your state's law of probate distribution. Then there's your *taxable estate* that includes those assets that the federal government or your state can tax. As you do estate planning, you need to appreciate the differences. Not everything in your estate is part of your probate estate, and not everything in your estate is subject to taxes.

✔ **Inventory all of your assets**

Before you can plan for the distribution of your estate you need to know what you own. Filling out all the checklists in the previous chapters is crucial to completing that inventory. And, assembling all that important information will be invaluable to your family because they will have to do it even if you have not. The more work you have done in inventorying what you have, the less time and effort they will have to expend in settling your financial affairs.

Your financial affairs will have to be settled by someone no matter how much planning you have done—or not done. The first step to setting your financial affairs at your death is to identify everything you own—bank accounts, investments, personal property, real estate—and everyone your owe—mortgages, debts, medical bills, funeral expenses. Then all your assets have to be categorized as to whether those assets are in your probate estate or are distributed outside of probate. Also your taxable assets, if any, have to be calculated.

It may sound like an oxymoron, but your probate estate includes everything that you have previously determined is not part of your probate estate. You take something out of your probate estate by owning property jointly with right of survivorship; by transferring property into a trust; and by indicating a beneficiary of your life insurance, annuity, investment account, or retirement fund. What is remaining is your probate estate. Your probate estate will be distributed according to the directions in your will or, if you have no will, according to the distribution laws in your state. If you have a will, you die *testate*; without a will you are said to have died *intestate*.

Probate

Probate is the court procedure that determines the validity of your will (if any), determines who will be in charge of settling your affairs, identifies your heirs, inventories your probate assets, determines claims against your estate, calculates any taxes to be paid, and distributes the remaining proceeds to the proper persons. By your will you determine who gets what and how much. If you don't have a will, your state's intestacy law does that for you. In effect, the probate court makes sure that your wishes or the law are carried out, supervises how your estate is distributed, adjudicates any disputes over the terms of your will or claims against your estate, and sorts out family disagreements.

✔ **Consult with a tax advisor**

✔ **Document any major financial gifts**

The IRS considers any gift to be taxable to you unless it falls within four specific exceptions.

- You can make gifts to your spouse without gift tax consequences
- You can make a gift of tuition or medical expenses for another if you pay the money directly to the institution or provider
- You can make annual gifts of less than $13,000 (in 2009)*
- You can make gifts to political organizations and qualifying charities

All other gifts for less than the item's fair market value should be reported to the IRS in the year you make the gift. The IRS considers the laws on gift taxes to be among the most complex in the tax code, so seek professional advice about how to handle any gifts—before you make the gift to avoid tax surprises. Nevertheless, your executor will need documentation of any gifts you have made during your lifetime to be able to calculate if any estate tax is due.

Gifts can also complicate your eligibility for Medicaid. Medicaid is another very complex area, primarily because the laws frequently change and because the details can vary from state to state. To simply summarize current law, before you can be eligible for Medicaid assistance in paying for your medical care in a long term care facility you will have to demonstrate that you have made no gifts ("transfers for less than fair market value") in the five years prior to your application for Medicaid. As with the gift tax laws, there are permissible ways to make gifts under Medicaid rules, but they are similarly complex. However, it is recommended that you get expert advice from an elder law attorney before making any gift.

*Note: As of this writing, Congress was revisiting gift and estate tax laws. Check with an estate planning or elder law attorney for current tax provisions.

✔ Discuss your estate plan with your executor

Executors and Administrators

If you have a will and have named the person you want to be in charge of managing your estate, the court will appoint that person as your ***executor***. If you have no will in which you nominate an executor, the court will appoint an ***administrator*** for you. The duties of your ***personal representative***, whether called an executor or administrator, are the same.

You should choose your executor with care because the person you name has many responsibilities. It can be a big task that requires good financial skills, attention to detail, patience, and probably a dose of diplomacy. Your personal representative must inventory your assets, have them appraised, pay bills, publish legal notices, prepare your final income tax return, work with financial institutions to close out accounts, record documents to sell or transfer real estate, find and notify beneficiaries, file any estate tax returns, and file inventories and accountings with the court. All the while your personal representative must keep happy the anxious and impatient debtors and beneficiaries of your estate.

✔ Identify a source of funding for any anticipated estate settlement fees

Costs and Fees

Much has been written about the cost of probate, with some suggesting that probate is a detrimental process that should be avoid at all costs. In reality, going through probate means same as settling your estate. Settling your estate does incur fees and costs that cannot be avoided, but you can control some of the expense through advance preparation and planning. Some minor costs of the probate process include filing fees to open the probate case by presenting your will and publishing legal notices in newspapers. Some states may also charge other filing fees for the inventory or accountings. The major expenses in settling your estate – with or without probate court involvement – are professional fees for an attorney, Realtor, appraiser, accountant, or tax preparer. The attorney for your estate advises your personal representative, assists in filing court documents, and represents your estate in any disputes. These professional fees will be paid as an expense of your estate. The more complex your financial affairs are, the higher your professional fees will be. Also the less clear your wishes, the higher the professional fees.

The other major expense is compensation for your personal representative. Depending on the laws of your state, your personal representative will be paid a percentage of the inventory value of your estate or a set fee determined by the judge. States that use a percentage to calculate the fee typically use a sliding scale. As the size of the estate increases, a smaller percentage is taken from the greater portions of the estate. For example, a personal representative might be entitled to a fee of 5 percent on the first $10,000 of an estate, 4 percent of the next $25,000, 3 percent of the next $50,000, and 2 percent of anything over $85,000.

In the other states the personal representative's fee is based on what would be "just and reasonable" compensation for the amount of work the representative has to do. The amount of work involved by two personal representatives can differ considerably even for estates of the same value. It is much simpler to administer an estate if assets can be readily found, no claims against the estate need to be resolved, and no family squabbles need to be negotiated. You can make your personal representative's job much easier—and less expensive to your estate—by completing the checklists in this book. The more advance work you do, the less time and expense your personal representative has to incur.

✔ Prepare or review your will

A will, or last will and testament, is the legal document by which you determine who you want to receive your probate property. If you have a friend or significant other who is not related to you that you want to receive any of your estate, you must have a will. By having a will you can also make sure that someone (other than your spouse) who would inherit if you don't have a will does not.

You should also name the person you want to be the executor of your estate. If you have minor children you need to name who you want to be their guardian until they reach the age of majority. If you wish to leave assets to any minors, such as your grandchildren, you are advised to create a testamentary trust so that their inheritance can be managed until they reach majority. A *testamentary trust*, unlike a living trust, is set up as part of your will and comes into effect after your death. You may also want to consider making donations to the charities, schools, or the religious groups that you support and take advantage of tax laws that encourage private philanthropy.

It is a good idea to review your will every few years, especially whenever the tax laws change. You may want to consult with your attorney or financial adviser to make sure your will continues to express your estate plan. Your personal or family circumstances may also have changed since you first drafted your will.

✔ Prepare any necessary codicils to your will

Codicil

A *codicil* is a document that amends your will. As circumstances change, such as a death, divorce or birth in your family, you may want to change a part of your will. You may need to add a bequest for a new grandchild, or change whom you want as your executor.

It can be easier to draft a codicil rather than rewriting and re-executing your entire will. However, this is not a do-it-yourself project. Do not make any changes directly on your will. Strike outs, erasures, and any other markings on your will can have the devious effect of invalidating your will. A codicil must be executed with the same formality, number of witnesses, and notary requirements as your will.

✔ Consider if a living trust should be part of your estate plan

A living trust is a legal arrangement in which you transfer your interest in property so it can be managed for you. It is called a living trust because you create it while you are still alive. The trustee you select has the responsibility to manage your trust assets while you are alive as well as after your death. In addition to creating the trust document, you must also "fund" the trust by preparing deeds, retitling assets, reassigning brokerage accounts or other steps to transfer ownership of the property you want in the trust. Because you must transfer legal ownership to the trust, the property in the trust no longer legally belongs to you and, therefore, is not part of your probate assets.

Every trust has three parties: the creator, the trustee, and the beneficiary or beneficiaries. But, the same individual can be all three at the same time. Many people who create a living trust (called a settlor, grantor, or donor) name themselves as the trustee because they want to manage the trust as long as they can. They also name a successor trustee who takes over the trust management when the settlor no long is willing or able to be the trustee and then after the settlor's death. You can also name yourself as the principal trust beneficiary so you can receive the trust proceeds to support yourself while you are alive. You would also name secondary beneficiaries with instructions on when and how the trust assets are to be held and distributed after your death. In this way your trust serves a very similar purpose to your will in identifying how any trust assets are distributed to the beneficiaries you have named. Because any assets you have transferred to the trust are not part of your probate estate, your trust, rather than your will, controls how those assets are distributed.

A trust can be an important component to your estate plan. Whether you should have a trust, in addition to your will, depends on many personal factors. If you have substantial property that you may not be able to manage if you become incapacitated, you may want to set up a trust. Having your assets managed by a trustee can avoid the need for the appointment of a guardian to oversee your estate if you become mentally or physically unable to do so yourself. By placing real estate that you own in another state into a trust, you may be able to avoid the need to go through the probate process in the other state.

You should discuss with your estate planner whether a trust would be appropriate in your circumstances and what assets might best be placed into a trust. Be sure to find out if placing your home in a living trust would jeopardize any homestead exemption, impact eligibility for Medicaid, or increase your property taxes. Putting property into a living trust does not reduce your income or estate taxes. It also does not protect your property from creditors. Because not all your property will be held by your trust, you will want to have a will to direct the distribution of any property that is not in your trust and that you have not otherwise planned for how it is to be inherited.

You may want to consider setting up a trust to provide for the care of your pets. According to the American Veterinary Medical Association, 44 states have adopted pet trust laws. These laws specifically allow you to name your pet as a beneficiary of a trust so you can ensure that funds are available for its care.

✔ **Select an agent to manage your financial affairs**

Power of Attorney

A power of attorney can be one of the most useful documents that you can prepare, but it is only effective during your lifetime. By creating a power of attorney you select the trustworthy individual – called your agent, or attorney-in-fact – you want to manage your financial affairs if you become unable to do so yourself. It can give you peace of mind that if something should happen to you, the person you choose will have the authority to act for you.

You can determine what responsibilities and duties you want your agent to have. You may want to give your agent general powers to do everything that you could do, or you may want to give specific powers. Among the powers that you can delegate to another are the reponsibility to manage your investments, pay your bills, collect your debts, sue on your behalf, sell your real estate, negotiate with insurance companies, sell your car, or have access to bank accounts. You may want your agent to sign your income tax returns, apply for benefits on your behalf, or make gifts to your favorite charities. If you want your agent to be able to make gifts, you need to be very specific about how those gifts are to be made. You should design your power of attorney to fit your anticipated needs.

Powers of attorney can differ depending on when you want your agent to be able to act for you. A ***durable*** power of attorney begins when you sign, but stays in effect for your lifetime—even after you become incapacitated—unless you cancel it. In most states you must put specific words in the document stating that you want your agent's powers to stay in effect even if you become incapacitated. If you want this feature, it's very important that you have these words in your document. In those states that have adopted the new Uniform Power of Attorney Act you do not need to be concerned about including the "durable" language; the law presumes that you want your agent to act after you become incapacitated.

You can also state in your power of attorney that you want to delay the time when you want your agent to begin to act. This is called a ***springing*** power of attorney because the effectiveness of the document springs into effect at some time after you have signed the document. Your attorney must carefully draft a springing power of attorney to avoid any difficulty in determining exactly when the springing event has happened.

Even if you sign a power of attorney, you can still manage your own affairs. You are not giving up anything. Think of a power of attorney as an extra set of car keys that you give to someone else. You have your own keys and determine when that extra set of keys can be used. When you can't or don't want to drive yourself, someone else has the keys to do the driving for you.

You can cancel, or revoke, a power of attorney at any time by tearing it up, by signing a new one, or by writing that you want to cancel it. You don't have to give any reason. If you do cancel, be sure to let your agent and anyone your agent has been dealing with know that you have cancelled your agent's authority.

All powers of attorney come to an end at your death. Your agent will have no authority to make any decisions after you die. Likewise, the executor you name in your will has no authority to act before your death.

Before deciding what powers you want your agent to have, you need carefully to consider whom you want to be your agent. Select someone you trust completely and who can do the job. It is best to avoid someone who is ill, inexperienced in financial matters, has a hard time managing their own money, or who for some other reason would not be able to carry out his or her responsibilities. Remember you are giving your agent the opportunity to access your funds at a time when you may not be able to keep tabs on what the agent is doing. You may want to add ways for other people to check up on what your agent is doing when you cannot.

If you want your agent to have access to your bank account, be sure to get your bank's authorization forms and a signature card for your agent. Typically a bank has its own form it wants your agent to sign before giving your agent access to a particular account. If you and your agent do not contact the bank before you become incapacitated, the bank may not honor checks or withdrawals your agent signs.

Giving your agent the authority to access your bank account is not the same as making someone a joint owner of the account. You'll want to make sure that you create the right kind of account so your agent has access to your funds to pay your bills but is not listed as an owner.

✔ Prepare a letter of instruction

A **letter of instruction** serves as guidance to your personal representative and your family about matters they must attend to after your death and how you want specific personal possessions divided.

This informal document can be attached to your will but is not an official part of it. You don't need an attorney to prepare it. Although it doesn't carry the legal weight of a will and is in no way a substitute for one, a letter of instruction clarifies any special requests you want your family to carry out when you die. Think of it as a flexible, informal supplement to your will that covers more personal information than what is typically included in a will. You can easily change it as your circumstances or wishes change. Just as with all your other estate planning documents, be sure your loved ones know where your letter of instruction is located.

Your letter of instructions can have two parts that do two different things. The first part helps your family know how to find the information necessary to plan your funeral. You might include instructions about the type of funeral or memorial service you want, who should officiate, whom you want as pall bearers, or what songs should—or should not—be sung. You need to let your family know about your plans with the funeral home and whether you have already paid for any of the arrangements. Describe the location of your pre-purchased burial plot or crypt and where you keep the plot deed. If you want to be cremated, your family needs to know where you want your ashes placed. Much of this information can be detailed in Chapter 10 of this book.

The other part of your letter of instruction may help eliminate any family feuds over who you want to receive your personal items. We all have heard stories of family fights erupting over how to divide family pictures, necklaces, the stamp collection, or the wedding gift from Aunt Sue. The items may not have monetary value, but getting them to the right person can make a big difference to you and to them.

If you want to make sure that your granddaughter gets the pearl necklace you got for your high school graduation, or your have already promised your best friend she gets your figurine collection, put your wishes in your letter. Be sure to leave instructions about care for your pets. If you have ideas or preferences as to who should get what, write it down.

You can make your letter personal, too. You can use it to send important messages to your survivors. You might include special hopes you have for your grandchild's education, or the important values you want to pass on. This could be the place to tell your family something you never got around to saying. It can be whatever you want it to be. You may want to consider also preparing an ethical will discussed on page 195.

Your wishes can change over time. It is easy to revisit your instructions every couple of years or when your circumstances change. You don't have to follow any legal format. Always sign and date each revision to eliminate confusion over which is your most current statement. Just make sure your latest instructions are clear.

Don't keep the document a secret! Don't put it in your safe deposit box where your family may not find it in time to plan your funeral.

Heirs Checklist

✔ If you have been given the responsibility to serve as someone's agent, know and appreciate the limitations of what you can and cannot do.

✔ Know where the will, codicil, and trust documents are located.

✔ Consult with an experienced probate attorney about probate procedures and requirements in your state.

CHAPTER 9
WILLS, TRUST AGREEMENTS, AND POWERS OF ATTORNEY CHECKLISTS

Codicils

☐   I have not executed any codicils.

☐   I have executed the following codicils:

Codicil date: _____

Executor (if changed):_____

Phone: _____ Email:_____

Address: _____

_____

Witness's name: _____

Phone: _____ Email:_____

Address: _____

_____

Witness's name: _____

Phone: _____ Email:_____

Address: _____

_____

Durable Power of Attorney

☐   I do not have a durable power of attorney for financial management.

☐   I do have a durable power of attorney for financial management.

Agent's name: _____

Phone: _____ Email: _____

Address: _____

_____

Gifts

☐   I have made no gifts in excess of $13,000.*

☐   I have made the following gifts in excess of $13,000:

Gift To Whom	Date	Gift	Value

* The annual gift exclusion changes from year to year. The exempt amount prior to 2002 was $10,000; for 2002-2005 it was $11,000; for 2006-2008 it was $12,000. For 2009 it was $13,000. At the time of this writing the rate for 2010 and beyond is unsettled.

.

Letter of Instruction

☐   I do not have a letter of instruction.

☐   I do have a letter of instruction.

My letter of instruction is located: _____

I last updated my letter of instruction on _____

Living Trust

☐ I do not have a living trust.

☐ I do have a living trust.

Trustee's name: _____

Phone: _____ Email: _____

Address: _____

_____

Witness's name: _____

Phone: _____ Email: _____

Address: _____

_____

Witness's name: _____

Phone: _____ Email: _____

Address: _____

_____

Will

☐ I do not have a will.

☐ I do have a will.

Attorney's name: _____

Phone: _____ Email: _____

Address: _____

_____

Witness's name: _____

Phone: _____ Email: _____

Address: _____

_____

Witness's name: _____

Phone: _____ Email: _____

Address: _____

_____

The original of my will is located: _____

Wills, Trust Agreements, and Powers of Attorneys: Other

The following miscellaneous information about my estate planning may be of interest to my heirs:

_____

_____

_____

_____

_____

_____

_____

_____

_____

_____

_____

_____

_____

_____

_____

_____

_____

_____

_____

_____

_____

_____

_____

_____

_____

_____

CHAPTER 10
FINAL WISHES

*Learn to wish that everything should come to pass
exactly as it does.*

— Epictetus

One of the kindest things that you can do for your family and heirs is to spare them the distress of facing decisions about your health care and your final arrangements without knowing your wishes. You can do this by making those decisions yourself and sharing them in this book.

Any time you become seriously ill—whatever your age—many decisions have to be made about the medical care that you receive. As long as you are able to communicate your wishes, health care providers look to you for answers about what treatment choices you want. In those situations when you cannot communicate your wishes, decisions still have to be made. Your family and health care providers want to respect your treatment preferences, but they need to know ahead of time how to make the decisions you want them to make. Advance care planning involves thinking about what treatments and health care you do or do not want, communicating your thoughts to those who will be called upon to make decisions on your behalf, and finally, putting those wishes down on paper in the appropriate legal forms.

In addition to knowing your wishes for your health care, your family needs to know your preferences for arrangements that should be made when you die. You have many options. You may want a simple ceremony that celebrates your life or a more elaborate memorial service. If you are a veteran, you may want a military bugler with burial in a national cemetery. Many people have firm opinions about whether a casket should be open or closed.

The many checklists in this book walk you through multiple options to help you decide what you do or do not want. By doing this advance planning now, your family won't have to guess. Also, if you have pre-paid for any part of your funeral or burial, your family needs to know about the contract so they don't have to pay unnecessarily for anything you have already paid for.

My Checklist

Done   **To Do**

Done	To Do	
☐	☐	Select the person you want to be your health care agent
☐	☐	Consider preparing an ethical will
☐	☐	Prepare an organ donor card
☐	☐	Plan the disposition of your body
☐	☐	Plan your funeral
☐	☐	Consider options for paying for your funeral
☐	☐	Plan your burial
☐	☐	Complete the checklists for Chapter 10

Final Wishes Checklists

The checklists in Chapter 10 are set out in the following order:

- *Burial*
- *Celebration of Life*
- *Charities*
- *Cremation*
- *Donation of Organs and Tissues*
- *Entombment*
- *Ethical Will/Legacy Documents*
- *Final Wishes*
- *Funeral*
- *Health Care Directives*
- *Living Will*
- *Items to Destroy*
- *Letters to Friends and Relatives*
- *Memorial Service*

- *Obituary*
- *People to Contact*
- *Pet Care*
- *Whole Body Donation*
- *Final Wishes: Other*

✔ **Select the person you want to be your health care agent**

Health care directives

An advance directive is a legally accepted means for you to convey to your family and doctor the types of care you would want in the event you are unable to communicate and who you want to make decisions about that care when you cannot.

Most people have heard of a **living will**, yet it's only half the legal instruction that makes up an advance directive. A living will outlines the treatments you would or would not want if you are unable to communicate and your death is imminent, or if you're permanently unconscious, in a vegetative state, or the end-stage of a chronic condition such as Alzheimer's disease. You may want to talk with your doctor about what are these life-limiting conditions.

In most states the law restricts the circumstances under which a living will is effective. Typically you can use it to document your wishes concerning specific end-of-life treatments. While it is crucial that your family and doctors understand your preferences concerning life-prolonging treatments, such as use of respirators, cardiopulmonary resuscitation, or intravenous nutrition or hydration, you may want to consider additional advance directives.

The second part of an advance directive is the selection of a health care agent who can speak for you if you are unable to do so. This is also referred to as appointing a health care proxy or signing a **durable power of attorney for health care**. In your advance directive you can give your agent broad authority to make any health care decision you specify, not about just life-prolonging treatments. You can set down any guidance or instructions you want your agent and your health care team to follow. And, perhaps more importantly, you have someone who will speak for you and get necessary information from your health care providers to make the decisions you would want to be made. By having your preferences in writing and someone to speak up on your behalf, you can help your family make difficult decisions and make sure your personal values are respected.

Your agent should be someone who knows you and understands your wishes about medical treatments. You can authorize him or her to make decisions in situations you might not have anticipated. Your agent can talk with your health care providers about your changing medical condition and authorize treatment or have it withdrawn as circumstances change. In the sometimes bewildering medical system it is good to have someone in charge who can advocate for you. If health care providers resist following your wishes, your agent can negotiate with them and take any other necessary steps to see that your wishes are honored. This includes changing doctors or hospitals if necessary to get the care you want.

When selecting your health care agent you should choose someone you trust and who will be there for you now and well into the future. You will need to feel comfortable talking with him or her about your end-of-life care and confident that he or she will follow your wishes even if they are not similar to their own. Your agent should be able to be assertive, if necessary, when talking with health care professionals. Your choice also needs to meet your state's criteria for health care agents. Most states exclude some categories of people who can serve as agents—such as your doctor, the administrator of the nursing home where you are residing, or someone who works in your nursing home.

The first step in preparing an advance directive is to have a conversation with yourself about what you may want for medical care in the future. For many, this is not a simple step. It can be hard to foresee what your medical needs or problems might be at some unknown point in the future. At this point you may want to talk with your family, doctor, spiritual advisors, or others who might be helpful in talking through serious medical issues and what brings quality to your life. The Five Wishes advance directive form may be helpful in starting and structuring important conversations about the medical care you wish to have. It is at www.agingwithdignity.org/five-wishes.php. The American Bar Association also has a kit that is very helpful in discussing with doctors and family your spiritual values, personal priorities, and more at www.abanet.org/aging/toolkit/.

The next step is preparing your advance directive. You don't need a lawyer to draft this document as many forms are available. You can find state-specific forms at www.caringinfo.org and links to other information about advance directives at new.abanet.org/aging/Pages/HealthDecisions.aspx. Many elder law attorneys provide advance directives of part of estate and health care planning. Most hospitals, area agencies on aging, bar associations or medical societies also provide free forms.

Perhaps even more important than signing the document is the conversations you want to have with your health care agent. Your agent needs to understand what is important to you for your quality of life and the kind of medical care you would or would not want to have. Think of your advance directive as a written record of the conversations you have had with your agent about the decisions you have made about your quality of life. Having your preferences in writing can be backup support for your agent and provide assurance that your wishes are known.

Your agent and your health care providers need to have copies of your advance directives. You may also wish to carry a wallet card that indicates you have an advance directive and how to get in touch with your agent.

✔ Consider preparing an ethical will

Ethical Will

Ethical wills may be one of the most cherished and meaningful gifts you can leave to your family. They are a way to share your values, blessings, life's lessons, hopes and dreams for the future, love and forgiveness with your family, friends, and future generations. Preparing an ethical will is an opportunity to put down on paper what you hold dear—your memories, insights and special wisdom that you don't want to be lost or forgotten. You may also want to make a video or audio recording of your ethical will as a cherished legacy for later generations.

Ethical wills are not new. They are an ancient tradition for passing on personal values, beliefs, blessings and advice to future generations. Initially, ethical wills were transmitted orally. Over time, they evolved into written documents. Ethical wills are not considered legal documents as compared to your living will and your last will and testament which are legal documents.

You can find examples of ethical wills at ethicalwill.com/examples.html with tips on how to get started preparing one.

Dr. Barry Baines, author of *Ethical Wills, Putting Your Values on Paper*, suggests the following personal reasons for writing an ethical will.

- We all want to be remembered, and we all will leave something behind.
- If we don't tell our stories, no one else will and they will be lost forever.
- It helps us identify what we value most and what we stand for.
- By articulating what we value now, we can take steps to ensure the continuation of those values for future generations.
- You learn a lot about yourself in the process of writing an ethical will.
- It helps us come to terms with our mortality by creating something of meaning that will live on after we are gone.
- It provides a sense of completion in our lives.

Final Arrangements

Your family will need to make many decisions at the time of your death. You will be giving them a precious gift if you relieve them of any uncertainty about your wishes. By indicating what you want and the plans you have in place on the checklists in this chapter, your family will be able to act with confidence that they are doing the right thing. For example, if you have already made arrangements with a medical school to donate your body for medical research or if you wish to be an organ donor, your family has to know your plans promptly upon your death. Decisions concerning the care of your body, including whether you want to be cremated or embalmed, also are time sensitive.

✔ Prepare an organ donor card

Do you wish to share the gift of your organs or tissues with someone needing a transplant? These donations have saved or improved thousands of lives. Yet there is always a very long list of patients waiting for organ transplants. According to the U.S. Department of Health and Human Services, 17 patients die each day because of the shortage of available donated organs.

If you do, you need to sign and carry an organ donation card. In some states you can indicate your wish to be an organ donor on your driver's license. Most, but not all, states have an organ donation registry. You can find out if your state does at www.organdonor. gov/donor/registry.shtm. It is easy to download a uniform donor form at ftp://ftp.hrsa.gov/organdonor/newdonorcard.pdf.

You and your family will not have any expenses related to your donation. Most organ donations are made after a person has been declared brain dead following an accident, heart attack, or stroke. The organs or tissues are removed through a surgical procedure. Most transplanted organs must be used within hours of the donation, while tissue donations of corneas, heart values, skin, and bones can be preserved and stored in tissue banks. After the removal procedures, your body can be buried or cremated as though it were intact.

If you wish to make a *whole body donation* to a medical school or research facility, you need to make arrangements with the school or research entity before you die. You can find a list of anatomical research programs at www.med.ufl.edu/anatbd/usprograms.html where you can learn more about what you need to do to make these arrangements. Be sure to talk with your family about your donation wish so they will know the specific instructions for how to transfer your body. Typically the facility will cremate your body at no expense and deliver your ashes as you instruct.

✔ Plan the disposition of your body

You will need to decide what you wish to have done with your body after your death. Your choices may include being embalmed to delay decomposition of your body, a natural burial without embalming, burial in a coffin in a cemetery or in a crypt in a mausoleum, or cremation. If you prefer cremation, your ashes may be buried in an urn at a cemetery, placed in a columbarium, or scattered at the location of your choice.

Every state has regulations concerning the scattering of ashes so check with your state agency that regulates burials. The scattering of ashes at sea must be done three nautical miles from land and the Environmental Protection Agency needs notice within thirty days of the burial.

More people are considering natural or "green" burials. With natural burial your body would not be embalmed and would be promptly buried in the ground in a biodegradable coffin made of cardboard or bamboo, or in a shroud. Other possible elements of a green burial could be to have a tree or shrub planted instead of a stone grave marker, or to request that instead of bouquets of cut flowers that gifts be made to your favorite charity.

Those of the Jewish faith have special rituals for the washing of the body, staying with the body until burial and prompt burial without embalming.

Because of the many options, be sure your family knows of your wishes.

✔ Plan your funeral

How do you wish your death to be commemorated? Depending on your family, cultural, or religious traditions, you may wish no service or ceremony, a lively gathering of family and friends to celebrate your life, a memorial service, a viewing at a mortuary, a wake, or a religious service in your place of worship. A funeral generally means that the body of the deceased is present, while a memorial service is held when the body has been buried or has been cremated.

A funeral director can assist you in planning for whatever type of commemoration you wish. You can discuss ahead of time the type of casket you would prefer, as well as other arrangements for any service or ceremony. Funeral directors must give your written price lists that tell you the costs for body preparation and transportation, caskets or urns, as well as other services. They can also help you make arrangements for the type of grave marker or headstone you prefer. Headstones typically extend above the ground to identify the person buried. Grave markers lay flat on the ground. Some cemeteries or memorial parks require grave markers to make it easier to care for the grounds. You should indicate on the Burial Checklist what inscription you want on your headstone or grave marker.

✔ Consider options for paying for your funeral

Pre-need contracts

Many funeral directors offer the option for you to pay a fixed price now for your funeral. An advantage of pre-paying includes fixing the costs at today's prices for your choice of a coffin and other services that may cost more in the future. Also, you can make the financial arrangements for your funeral expenses to give you the peace of mind that your family will not have this financial burden.

Before pre-paying for your funeral with a funeral director, get confirmation in writing about how your financial investment will be protected. You want to be assured that your money is in safe hands and your pre-need contract will be honored as much as a decade or two in the future. With most pre-need contracts you turn over a sum of money, either a lump sum or in installment payments. Your money is then placed in trust held by a third-party trustee or used to purchase an insurance policy. The trustee or insurance company is responsible to manage the money until it is time to pay the funeral home for the goods and services you listed in your contract. Inquire whether your funds will be securely placed in a trust held by a financially sound third-party or used to purchase an insurance policy.

You will also want to inquire about the portability of your contract if you should move to another location and no longer want your funeral where you used to live. If your plans change or the funeral home changes hands, you'll want to be able to transfer the contract. Before paying for a pre-need contract, check with your state's attorney general or board of funeral directors to learn how pre-need contracts are regulated in your state. Your family will need to know if you have a pre-need contract so include the details on the Funeral Checklist.

There are other options for making sure your family is not saddled with the expenses for your funeral. You may wish to purchase a life insurance policy that would cover the anticipated funeral costs. You could invest your money in a certificate of deposit or in a savings account designated to cover these expenses. With options like these you will know that the money will be available to your family, but you remain in control of the money as your plans for your final arrangements change.

✔ Plan your burial

If you wish your body to be buried you will need to purchase a lot at a cemetery or a niche in a mausoleum. You can purchase just a single lot or a number of lots in a block where other family members would also be buried. When purchasing a cemetery lot you should inquire about any additional charges for opening and closing the grave site and for the perpetual care of the site. You should receive a deed to the land, or plot, that you have purchased. The cost of cemetery lots varies significantly depending on where you wish to be buried. It is essential that your family knows if you have purchased a cemetery plot or crypt in a mausoleum so they can make the correct arrangements.

Heirs Checklist

✔ If you have been selected to be the health care agent, be confident that you know the answers to these questions:

  • What aspects of their life give it the most meaning?

- How their religious or spiritual beliefs affect their attitudes toward end-of-life care?
- What is their attitude towards death or the dying process?
- Whether they prefer to die at home if possible?
- Are there certain treatments they would want or would refuse? Under what conditions?
- Would they consider certain treatments on a trial basis?

✔ Read the ABA's *Legal Guide for the Seriously Ill: Seven Key Steps to Get Your Affairs in Order*.

www.caringinfo.org/UserFiles/File/PDFs/AdvanceCarePlanningLegalIssues/Legal_Guide_for_Seriously_Ill.pdf.

✔ Know whether your loved one wishes to be an organ or tissue donor or has made arrangements to donate his or her body for medical or scientific research. Under most state laws, a surviving spouse, or if there is no surviving spouse a specific priority list of relatives, may make the donation if there is no consent documentation.

✔ Review with your loved one as far in advance as possible his or her wishes for a funeral, memorial service, burial, or cremation.

✔ Know where to find any cemetery deed and pre-need funeral contract. Review the terms of the pre-need contract so you understand what is and is not covered.

CHAPTER 10
FINAL WISHES CHECKLISTS

Burial

☐ I do not wish to be buried.

☐ I do wish to be buried.

☐ I do not own a cemetery lot.

☐ I do own a cemetery lot.

The ownership of the lot is in the name of: _____

The lot is located at:

Cemetery: _____

Section: _____ Lot: _____

Address: _____

_____

Other description:

_____

_____

Location of deed: _____

☐ I do not own a crypt in a mausoleum or columbarium.

☐ I do own the following crypt:

The ownership of the crypt is in the name of: _____

The crypt is located at:

Name: _____

Address: _____

_____

Space #:_____

Other description:

_____

_____

Location of deed or contract: _____

☐ I would like to have a grave marker.

☐ I would like to have a grave marker furnished by the Department of Veterans Affairs.

☐ I would like to have a service medallion furnished by the Department of Veterans Affairs.

I would like the following words to be placed on it:

_____

_____

Other instructions:

_____

_____

_____

Celebration of Life

- ☐ I do not want a celebration of life ceremony.
- ☐ I do want a celebration of life ceremony.
- ☐ I have made prearrangements for a celebration of life ceremony.

Type of celebration: _____

People to invite:

_____
_____
_____
_____
_____
_____

Arrangement details:

Place: _____

Time: _____

Serving suggestions:

_____
_____
_____
_____
_____

Entertainment suggestions:

_____
_____

_____

_____

☐ I have created music for the event.

☐ I have created a video for the event.

☐ I have created other for the event: _____

Charities

☐   I do not want any memorial donations or gifts to charities.

☐   I would appreciate memorial donations or gifts to the following charities:

Charity Name	Charity Address	Charity Phone	Charity Contact	Connection

Cremation

- ☐ I wish my body to be cremated.
- ☐ I wish my body to be cremated followed by a memorial service.
- ☐ I wish my body to be cremated followed by a celebration of life service.

Following my cremation, I wish my ashes to be disbursed as follows:

- ☐ To be scattered:

  _____

- ☐ To be placed in an urn and buried or entombed:

  _____

- ☐ Other:

  _____

- ☐ To be handled as my heirs see fit.

*****

- ☐ I have not made prearrangements for my cremation.
- ☐ I have made the following prearrangements for my cremation:

Company: _____

Address: _____

_____

Phone: _____ Website: _____

The contract is located: _____

Donation of Organs and Tissues

☐ I do not wish to donate any organs or tissues.

☐ I wish to donate any needed organs or tissues.

☐ I wish to donate only the following organs or tissues:

Organs:

☐ Heart

☐ Kidneys

☐ Liver

☐ Lungs

☐ Pancreas

☐ Other_____

Tissues:

☐ Blood vessels

☐ Bone

☐ Cartilage

☐ Corneas

☐ Heart valves

☐ Inner ear

☐ Intestines

☐ Skin

☐ Other_____

****

☐ I have not executed a uniform donor card.

☐ I have executed a uniform donor card.

☐ I have registered with my state's organ donation registry.

My uniform donor card is located: _____

207

Entombment

☐   I do not wish to be entombed.

☐   I do wish to be entombed.

☐   I do not own a crypt.

☐   I do own crypt.

The ownership of the crypt is in the name of: _____

The mausoleum is located at:

Cemetery: _____

Section: _____ Crypt: _____

Address: _____

_____

Other description:

_____

_____

Location of deed: _____

☐   I would like to have a marker.

I would like the following words to be placed on it:

_____

_____

Other instructions:

_____

_____

_____

_____

_____

_____

Ethical Will/Legacy Documents

    ☐   I have not created any legacy documents.

    ☐   I have created an ethical will.

    ☐   I have created the following legacy documents:

Ethical will:

_____

_____

_____

Books:

_____

_____

_____

Pamphlets:

_____

_____

_____

Videos:

_____

_____

_____

Other:

_____

_____

_____

Please distribute them as follows:

_____

_____

_____

Final Wishes

I wish my body to:

- ☐ Become an organ donor
- ☐ Be bequeathed to a medical school
- ☐ Be buried in the earth
- ☐ Be entombed in a mausoleum
- ☐ Be cremated
- ☐ Other: _____

*****

I wish to have:

- ☐ A funeral service (body present)
- ☐ A memorial service (body not present)
- ☐ A celebration of life service
- ☐ No service
- ☐ I would like an American flag covering my coffin
- ☐ I would like to have military funeral honors
- ☐ Other: _____

*****

My preferences are as follows:

House of worship:

_____

_____

_____

_____

Religious leader or speakers at services:

_____

_____

_____

_____

Funeral home:

_____

_____

_____

_____

Memorial society:

_____

_____

_____

_____

Memorial donation requests:

_____

_____

_____

_____

Other:

_____

_____

_____

_____

Funeral

☐ I do not want a funeral.

☐ I do want a funeral.

I wish the service to be for:

☐ Friends and relatives

☐ Private

☐ Other: _____

I wish the casket to be:

☐ Closed

☐ Open

☐ I prefer to wear: _____

My favorite hymns, poems, and music:

_____

_____

_____

_____

My favorite flowers:

_____

_____

☐ I have not made funeral prearrangements.

☐ I have a pre-need contract and have pre-paid for some or all of my funeral.

☐ I have made the following funeral prearrangements:

Funeral home: _____

Address: _____

_____

Phone: _____

The pre-need contract is located: _____

Health Care Directives

☐ I do not have a durable power of attorney for health care.

☐ I do have a durable power of attorney for health care.

Health Care Agent's name: _____

Phone: _____ Email: _____

Address: _____

_____

My advance health care directive is located: _____

Living Will

☐ I do not have a living will.

☐ I do have a living will.

My living will is located: _____

Items to Destroy

Please destroy the following documents upon my death:

☐ _____

_____

_____

Location: _____

☐ _____

_____

_____

Location: _____

☐ _____

_____

_____

Location: _____

☐ _____

_____

_____

Location: _____

Letters to Friends and Relatives

☐   I do not have any letters for friends or relatives.

☐   I do have letters for friends and relatives as follows:

Person:_____

Address: _____

_____

Letter location: _____

Person:_____

Address: _____

_____

Letter location: _____

Person:_____

Address: _____

_____

Letter location: _____

Person:_____

Address: _____

_____

Letter location: _____

Memorial Service

☐　I do not want a memorial service.

☐　I do want a memorial service.

*****

I wish the service to be for:

☐　Friends and relatives

☐　Private

☐　Other: _____

*****

My favorite hymns, poems, and music:

_____

_____

_____

_____

My favorite flowers:

_____

_____

*****

☐　I have not made memorial service prearrangements.

☐　I have made the following memorial service prearrangements:

Funeral home: _____

Address: _____

_____

Phone: _____

Obituary

☐   I have written my own obituary.

My obituary is located: _____

I would like my obituary to appear in the following newspapers:

_____

_____

_____

I would like the following information to appear in my obituary:

_____

_____

_____

_____

_____

_____

_____

_____

People to Contact

I wish that the following people be contacted to let them know of my death:

Name: _____

Relationship: _____

Phone: _____ Email: _____

Address: _____

_____

Name: _____

Relationship: _____

Phone: _____ Email: _____

Address: _____

_____

Name: _____

Relationship: _____

Phone: _____ Email: _____

Address: _____

_____

Name: _____

Relationship: _____

Phone: _____ Email: _____

Address: _____

_____

Name: _____

Relationship: _____

Phone: _____ Email: _____

Address: _____

_____

Name: _____

Relationship: _____

Phone: _____ Email: _____

Address: _____

_____

Name: _____

Relationship: _____

Phone: _____ Email: _____

Address: _____

_____

Name: _____

Relationship: _____

Phone: _____ Email: _____

Address: _____

_____

Name: _____

Relationship: _____

Phone: _____ Email: _____

Address: _____

_____

Name: _____

Relationship: _____

Phone: _____ Email: _____

Address: _____

_____

Name: _____

Relationship: _____

Phone: _____ Email: _____

Address: _____

_____

Pet Care

- ☐ I do not have any pets.
- ☐ I have not made arrangements for the care of my pets.
- ☐ I have made arrangements for the care of my pets.
- ☐ I have not made financial arrangements for the care of my pets.
- ☐ I have made financial arrangements for the care of my pets.

I have made the following arrangements for the care of my pets:

_____

_____

_____

_____

_____

_____

_____

_____

I have made the following financial arrangements for the care of my pets:

_____

_____

_____

_____

_____

Whole Body Donation

☐ I wish to donate my body to the following:

Medical school:_____

Address: _____

_____

Phone: _____

Contact person: _____

Research organization: _____

Address: _____

_____

Phone: _____

Contact person: _____

☐ I have not made prearrangements with the above medical school or research organization.

☐ I have made prearrangements with the above medical school or research organization.

Final Wishes: Other

The following miscellaneous information about my final wishes may be of interest to my heirs:

_____

_____

_____

_____

_____

_____

_____

_____

_____

_____

_____

_____

_____

_____

_____

_____

_____

_____

_____

_____

_____

_____

APPENDIX A
CHECKLISTS

- *Checklist of Checklists*
- *My Checklist*
- *Survivors Checklist*
- *Heirs Checklist*

Checklist of Checklists

I have completed the following forms for my heirs and survivors:

Personal History

- ☐ Awards
- ☐ Biography
- ☐ Contacts
- ☐ Educational History
- ☐ Memberships
- ☐ Passwords
- ☐ Personal Medication Record
- ☐ Pets
- ☐ Records
- ☐ Religion, Politics, and Hobbies
- ☐ Residences
- ☐ Taxes
- ☐ Work History
- ☐ Personal History: Other

Family History

- ☐ Personal History
- ☐ Children
- ☐ Parents
- ☐ Brothers and Sisters
- ☐ Grandparents
- ☐ Aunts, Uncles, and Cousins
- ☐ Stepparents
- ☐ Stepbrothers and sisters
- ☐ Family Medical History
- ☐ Family History: Other

Insurance

- ☐ Annuity
- ☐ Automobile Insurance
- ☐ Health Insurance: Disability, Medicare, Long-Term Care
- ☐ Homeowners Insurance
- ☐ Life Insurance
- ☐ Other Residence Insurance
- ☐ Umbrella Policy Insurance
- ☐ Vehicle Insurance
- ☐ Insurance: Other

Benefits for Survivors

- ☐ Pensions
- ☐ Retirement Plans
- ☐ Social Security Benefits
- ☐ Veterans Benefits
- ☐ Workers' Compensation
- ☐ Benefits: Other

Banking and Savings

- ☐ Certificates of Deposit
- ☐ Checking Accounts
- ☐ Credit Unions
- ☐ Safe Deposit Boxes
- ☐ Savings Accounts
- ☐ Savings Bonds
- ☐ Banking and Savings: Other

Investments

- ☐ Bonds
- ☐ Money Market Funds and Accounts
- ☐ Mutual Funds
- ☐ Stocks
- ☐ Investments: Other

Real Estate

- ☐ Commercial
- ☐ Condominium
- ☐ Farm Land
- ☐ Residence
- ☐ Timeshares
- ☐ Real Estate: Other

Other Assets and Debts

- ☐ Business Interests
- ☐ Copyrights, Patents, Royalties, and Trusts
- ☐ Credit Cards
- ☐ Debts
- ☐ Lawsuits and Judgments
- ☐ Personal Property
- ☐ Reverse Mortgage
- ☐ Assets and Debts: Other

Wills, Trust Agreements, and Powers of Attorney

- ☐ Codicils
- ☐ Durable Power of Attorney
- ☐ Gifts
- ☐ Letter of Instruction
- ☐ Living Trust
- ☐ Will
- ☐ Wills, Trust Agreements, and Powers of Attorney: Other

Final Wishes

- ☐ Burial
- ☐ Celebration of Life
- ☐ Charities
- ☐ Cremation
- ☐ Donation of Organs and Tissues
- ☐ Entombment
- ☐ Ethical Will/Legacy Documents
- ☐ Final Wishes
- ☐ Funeral
- ☐ Health Care Directives
- ☐ Items to Destroy
- ☐ Living Will
- ☐ Letters to Friends and Relatives
- ☐ Memorial Service
- ☐ Obituary
- ☐ People to Contact
- ☐ Pet Care
- ☐ Whole Body Donation
- ☐ Final Wishes: Other

My Checklist

Personal History

- ✔ Get copies of birth certificate
- ✔ Get copies of marriage license
- ✔ Get copies of divorce decree
- ✔ Complete Personal Medication Record
- ✔ Organize tax files by year
- ✔ List all employers
- ✔ Keep original documents that are valuable or irreplaceable in a safe deposit box

Family History

- ✔ Take advantage of family gatherings or reunions to get help compiling family history information
- ✔ Complete Family Medical History

Insurance

- ✔ Review terms of all insurance policies
- ✔ Locate all insurance policies
- ✔ Review the beneficiaries on any life insurance policy
- ✔ Annually review your health insurance options

Benefits for Survivors

- ✔ Apply for Social Security benefits
- ✔ Apply for veterans benefits
- ✔ Get a copy of military service record
- ✔ Apply for workers' compensation
- ✔ Identify all available pension benefits
- ✔ Manage disbursement from your retirement plans
- ✔ Verify the beneficiary designation on pension or retirement plans

Banking and Saving

- ✔ Review how bank accounts are titled
- ✔ List all banks where you do business

- ✔ Assemble account numbers, and **with caution** your access PINs, ATM passwords, online banking usernames and passwords
- ✔ Keep a record of all savings bonds
- ✔ Make sure that your accounts are FDIC insured
- ✔ Keep original documents that are valuable or irreplaceable in a safe deposit box
- ✔ Be sure that someone knows where safe deposit boxes and keys are located
- ✔ List any credit unions where you do business

Investments

- ✔ Periodically check to make sure that your investments match your investment objectives and are diversified
- ✔ Check on the background and qualifications of your financial professional
- ✔ Organize statements you receive from your brokerage or investment adviser

Real Estate

- ✔ Assemble copies of the deeds to all real estate
- ✔ Review how your property is titled
- ✔ Discuss your real estate ownership and taxes with a tax adviser or estate planner
- ✔ Determine if your property qualifies for tax relief
- ✔ Consolidate all commercial property records
- ✔ Obtain a copy of your condominium's Master Deed and association documents
- ✔ Consolidate all farm land records
- ✔ Obtain a copy of your timeshare contract

Other Assets and Debts

- ✔ Assemble receipts or appraisals for higher-valued possessions
- ✔ Photograph or videotape special possessions
- ✔ Write down stories about how you acquired special possessions
- ✔ Put the terms of any personals loans in writing
- ✔ List contact information for credit cards
- ✔ Consider whether a reverse mortgage would be appropriate

Wills, Trust Agreements, and Powers of Attorney

- ✔ Consult with an estate planning expert
- ✔ Inventory all of your assets
- ✔ Consult with a tax advisor
- ✔ Document any major financial gifts
- ✔ Discuss your estate plan with your executor
- ✔ Identify a source of funding for any anticipated estate settlement fees
- ✔ Prepare or review your will
- ✔ Prepare any necessary codicils to your will
- ✔ Consider if a living trust should be part of your estate plan
- ✔ Select an agent to manage your financial affairs
- ✔ Prepare a letter of instruction

Final Wishes

- ✔ Select the person you want to be your health care agent
- ✔ Consider preparing an ethical will
- ✔ Prepare an organ donor card
- ✔ Plan the disposition of your body
- ✔ Plan your funeral
- ✔ Consider options for paying for your funeral
- ✔ Plan your burial

Survivors Checklist

Step 1:	What to do at time of death:	Refer to these checklists
☐	Authorize donation of organs or tissue.	Donation of Organs and Tissues
☐	Contact medical school for body bequeathal.	Whole Body Donation
☐	Contact funeral home for removal of body.	Final Wishes
☐	Notify contacts in appointment book and cancel appointments.	Records
☐	Ensure safety of real estate and property.	Real Estate, Homeowners Insurance
☐	Ensure safety of children and pets.	Pet Care
Step 2:	What to do *before* funeral or memorial service:	
☐	Contact funeral director or memorial society for arrangements.	Final Wishes
☐	Notify contacts (friends, relatives, employer, service providers, etc.) of funeral arrangements, donations, and charitable requests.	People to Contact
☐	Maintain a list of flowers, cards, donations, charities, and other expressions of sympathy.	
☐	Arrange for friends and relatives to help with childcare, shopping, cooking, telephones, etc.	
☐	Arrange for friends and relatives to help with pet care.	Pet Care
☐	Arrange funeral, memorial service, or private viewing.	Final Wishes
☐	Arrange for cemetery lot, mausoleum, or crypt.	Burial
☐	Arrange for Veteran's burial benefits, grave marker.	Veteran's Benefits
☐	Provide obituary information to newspaper.	Obituary
☐	Arrange for creation and printing of legacy information.	Ethical Will

☐	Arrange for after-service luncheon, celebration of life event, or other gathering for friends and relatives.	Celebration of Life
☐	Obtain a minimum of eight certified copies of death certificates.	
Step 3:	**What to do after funeral or memorial service:**	
☐	Send notes to acknowledge expressions of sympathy and donations.	
☐	Notify life insurance companies and file claim forms.	Life Insurance
☐	Notify other insurance providers and file claims where applicable.	Insurance
☐	Apply for appropriate Social Security survivors' benefits.	Social Security Benefits
☐	Apply for appropriate veteran's survivors' benefits.	Veteran's Benefits
☐	Meet with attorney to begin probate proceedings. Take original will and/or trust agreement and a copy of this book.	Will
☐	Assist with inventory of assets.	Other Assets and Debts Banking Investments Real Estate
☐	Notify accountant/tax preparer (unless estate lawyer is preparing final tax returns). Take copies of appropriate checklists in this book and copies of recent tax returns.	Records
☐	Notify financial advisor(s)/stockbroker(s) to change ownership of joint investment accounts.	Investments
☐	Suspend any open brokerage orders of the decedent.	Investments

☐	Notify bankers to change ownership of joint accounts.	Banking
☐	Cancel online banking accounts.	Checking Accounts Savings Accounts Credit Unions
☐	Inventory safe deposit boxes.	Safe Deposit Boxes
☐	Notify reverse mortgage company.	Reverse Mortgage
☐	Cancel driver's license.	
☐	Cancel email and website accounts.	Passwords
☐	Notify credit card companies. Close accounts and destroy cards.	Credit Cards
☐	Notify credit reporting companies.	Credit Cards
☐	Notify mail carrier and Post Office to forward mail.	
☐	Notify membership organizations, etc. to remove name of decedent.	Personal History
☐	Contact airlines to apply for transfer of frequent flyer miles to primary beneficiary.	Personal Property
☐	Arrange for headstone.	Final Wishes

Other _____

_____

Heirs Checklist

Personal History

- ✔ Offer to help to track down information, organize mementos, or create scrapbooks.
- ✔ Assist with keeping the Personal Medication Record up to date as medications change.

Family History

- ✔ Help dig into family history by offering to sort through photographs, letters, trunks and boxes in the attic.
- ✔ Try out some of the genealogical resources online to map out family trees.
- ✔ Offer to record on tape or video special memories to preserve oral family stories.

Insurance

- ✔ Immediately contact the insurance agent to ensure that the home and its contents are properly insured during the administration of the estate.
- ✔ Make sure that a homeowners' policy remains in effect if no one is going to be living in the residence during an extended nursing home stay or following the death of the homeowner.
- ✔ Contact the insurance company for instructions on how to file a claim for life insurance benefits.
- ✔ Notify the vehicle insurance company so there will complete coverage until the vehicle is sold or transferred to its next owner.

Benefits for Survivors

- ✔ Notify Social Security of the death
- ✔ Apply for Social Security survivor's benefits
- ✔ Apply for Social Security survivor's benefits as a former spouse
- ✔ Apply for Social Security benefits for and dependent children
- ✔ Apply for Medicare as an eligible spouse
- ✔ Apply for veterans burial benefits
- ✔ Get a copy of the veteran's service record
- ✔ Obtain a flag
- ✔ Apply for burial benefits

- ✔ Contact your local VA office
- ✔ Apply for veterans survivor's benefits
- ✔ Apply for workers' compensation survivor's benefits
- ✔ Apply for pension benefits for survivors
- ✔ Take disbursements from retirement plans

Banking and Savings

- ✔ Be sure you know where the keys to any safe deposit boxes are located.
- ✔ Notify all banks or credit unions of the death and provide a copy of the death certificate.
- ✔ Some bank accounts may be temporarily frozen to make certain that no improper withdrawals are made before the estate is settled.
- ✔ Any Social Security check that is received in the month of the individual's death must be returned un-cashed to Social Security.

Investments

- ✔ Promptly contact any investment professionals so that accounts can be valued as of the date of death for tax purposes.
- ✔ Notify any financial advisors or stock brokers to change ownership of joint investment accounts.
- ✔ Suspend any open brokerage orders.

Real Estate

- ✔ Secure all property for safety and sure it is insured.
- ✔ Change any locks as necessary.
- ✔ Consider notifying law enforcement to keep an eye on the property if the property will remain vacant for any period of time.
- ✔ Consult with an attorney about the need to change the title to any property if you are a surviving joint owner.
- ✔ Consult with an attorney about the rights you have as a survivor with respect to condominium property or timeshares.

Other Assets and Debts

- ✔ Notify the company servicing any reverse mortgage as soon as possible to make arrangement to pay off the loan. Interest continues to accrue until the loan is paid off so it is important to act quickly.

✔ Read *Borrowing Against Your Home* at http://www.aarp.org/revmort under "Resources" for more information about what you need to do to pay off a reverse mortgage.

✔ Notify all credit card companies and each credit reporting company (Experian, TransUnion and Equifax) so they can flag the accounts that the owner is deceased. This can help limit the opportunity for identity theft of the deceased person's credit information.

✔ Offer to help photograph or videotape special personal possessions.

Wills, Trust Agreements, and Powers of Attorney

✔ If you have been given the responsibility to serve as someone's agent, know and appreciate the limitations of what you can and cannot do.

✔ Know where the will, codicil, and trust documents are located.

✔ Consult with an experienced probate attorney about probate procedures and requirements in your state.

Final Wishes

✔ If you have been selected to be the health care agent, be confident that you know the answers to these questions:

- What aspects of their life give it the most meaning?
- How their religious or spiritual beliefs affect their attitudes toward end-of-life care?
- What is their attitude towards death or the dying process?
- Whether they prefer to die at home if possible?
- Are there certain treatments they would want or would refuse? Under what conditions?
- Would they consider certain treatments on a trial basis?

✔ Read the ABA's *Legal Guide for the Seriously Ill: Seven Key Steps to Get Your Affairs in Order*

www.caringinfo.org/UserFiles/File/PDFs/AdvanceCarePlanningLegalIssues/Legal_Guide_for_Seriously_Ill.pdf.

✔ Know whether your loved one wishes to be an organ or tissue donor or has made arrangements to donate his or her body for medical or scientific research. Under most state laws, a surviving spouse, or if there is no surviving spouse a specific priority list of relatives, may make the donation if there is no consent documentation.

✔ Review with your loved one as far in advance as possible his or her wishes for a funeral, memorial service, burial, or cremation.

✔ Know where to find any cemetery deed and preneed funeral contract. Review the terms of the preneed contract so you understand what is and is not covered.

APPENDIX B
RESOURCES

- *Books*
- *Websites*

Books

AARP Crash Course in Estate Planning: the Essential Guide to Wills, Trusts, and Your Personal Legacy. Michael T. Palermo, 2005. Published by Sterling Publishing Co.

All Together Now. Elaine Todd and Allan D. Schultz, 1997. Published by Blazing Star Press.

American Bar Association Guide to Wills and Estates, Third Edition. American Bar Association, 2009. Published by Random House.

Before It's Too Late, Third Edition. Emily Oishi and Sue Thompson, 2008. Published by Thompson.

Ethical Wills: Putting Your Values on Paper. Barry K. Baines, 2002. Published by Da Capo Press.

Get It Together. Melanie Cullen, 2008. Published by NOLO.

Legal Guide for the Seriously Ill: Seven Key Steps to Get Your Affairs in Order. American Bar Association Commission on Law and Aging, 2009. www.caringinfo.org/UserFiles/File/PDFs/AdvanceCarePlanningLegalIssues/Legal_Guide_for_Seriously_Ill.pdf

So That Your Values Live On: Ethical Wills and How to Prepare Them. Jack Riemer & Nathaniel Stampfer, 1991. Published by Jewish Lights Publishing.

The Measure of Our Success: A Letter to My Children and Yours. Marion Wright Edelman, 1993. Published by HarperPerennial.

Websites

AARP, www.aarp.org

Aging with Dignity, www.agingwithdignity.org

American Institute of CPAs, www.aicpa.org

American Bar Association, www.abanet.org

Caring Connections, www.caringinfo.org

Centers for Medicare and Medicaid Services, www.medicare.gov

Department of Veterans Affairs, www.va.gov

Financial Planning Association, www.fpanet.org

Five Wishes, www.agingwithdignity.org/five-wishes.php

National Academy of Elder Law Attorneys, www.naela.org

National Association of Estate Planners, www.naepc.org

National Association of Professional Geriatric Care Managers, www.caremanager.org

National Guardianship Association, www.guardianship.org

Senior Lawyers Division, www.abanet.org/srlawyer

Social Security Administration, www.ssa.gov

Funeral Consumer Alliance, www.funerals.org